SOUL
INSPIRATIONS
A Journey for the Divine

SOUL
INSPIRATIONS
A Journey for the Divine

KIANA LASHAYIA

PRIMIX
PUBLISHING
THE WRITE CHOICE

Primix Publishing
11620 Wilshire Blvd
Suite 900, West Wilshire Center, Los Angeles, CA, 90025
www.primixpublishing.com
Phone: 1-800-538-5788

Published by Primix Publishing   05/10/2022

ISBN: 978-1-955944-27-4(sc)
ISBN: 978-1-955944-28-1(e)

Library of Congress Control Number: 2021921298

Daily Poetry Readings

Strength

Perseverance

Patience

Praise

Hope

Peace

Love

Relationships

Prayer

Psalms 112

1   *Praise ye the Lord. Blessed is the man that feareth the Lord, that delighteth greatly in his commandments.*

2   *His seed shall be mighty upon earth: the generation of the upright shall be blessed.*`

3   *Wealth and riches shall be in his house: and his righteousness endureth for ever.*

4   *Unto the upright there ariseth light in the darkness: he is gracious, and full of compassion, and righteous.*

5   *A good man sheweth favour, and lendeth: he will guide his affairs with discretion.*

6   *Surely he shall not be moved for ever: the righteous shall be in everlasting remembrance.*

7   *He shall not be afraid of evil tidings: his heart is fixed, trusting in the Lord.*

8   *His heart is established, he shall not be afraid, until he see his desire upon his enemies.*

9   *He hath dispersed, he hath given to the poor; his righteousness endureth for ever; his horn shall be exalted with honour.*

10 *The wicked shall see it, and be grieved; he shall gnash with his teeth, and melt away: the desire of the wicked shall perish.*

"The best thing you can do for a person is to inspire them. That's the best currency you can offer: inspiration. So, when a person can rely on you for that, that empowers them in every realm of their life."
- Nipsey Hussle

PROLOGUE

Hi, I'm Kiana.

When I started writing my book I had no idea how it would finish, let alone start. I wanted to release my poetry in a different form, that could make people feel like they knew me personally. So I figured I would give a little insight to who Kiana LaShayia is. I find it most amusing how you can share many experiences in life, yet we all find various ways to overcome our situations. Several individuals stay in the dwelling place of downs, versus the ups, in this journey we tread. As for me, I choose to share my poetic truths through this book.

We all find inspiration in someone or something, and like others around the world, I discovered my motivations in someones like TD Jakes, Maya Angelou, and Oprah. My something was the church, which leads to my love of dance and singing. Thank God, He created outlets of expression to fight depression.

As you will see beyond these pages, I am a person who has doubts, fears, and worries, but I also have faith, hope, and power! Through the journey of my twenties, I have acquired much wisdom on the topics of life, and I know it to be true. Therefore, I take it as my responsibility to encourage and enlighten my peers, of the next generation to strive for change openly, as we transpire through life. Moreover, in the process, avoid recurrences of disappointment, loss, loneliness, hardships, and unforgiveness. I do believe bad times are inevitable, negative energy serves every bit of purpose, like the good or positive. It's not a fun lesson to learn, but it has its perks when you come out on the other side.

Patience has advanced, as a virtue of mine, with the addition of forgiveness.

These two words have become daily exercises for me, testing me regularly. I now see the world with new eyes. God has a fantastic way of changing your heart, and molding the mind. I have my opinions on the roads of those upon this earth, which could create a better place, for us all. That's why I choose to share them with the world by writing them and displaying them.

I've learned the power of my words, and I have discovered how to speak life over death with my tongue. When I chose to write my first inspiration poem, I never knew the Lord was building me up in my low times to encourage others. One day I woke up and realized people connected to the currents of my words. My words and thoughts had inclined a well of life to strangers, family, and friends. It's a humbling experience to be acknowledged beyond beauty, yet admired for my gifts, and a heart that truly yearns for my risen savior, Jesus.

I've often thought of myself as David from the Bible. Every time I would sit and read, or hear sermons about his character, I saw myself. Ironic how there is nothing new under the sun, that we could learn from others; therefore our Lord would put a series of stories together for our guide. I am an obvious fan of the Bible and the church. Blessed is the highest God, for sending me to church homes, that taught me who God is, and why he loves us so. I was brought up to believe that God is love, and when I read the word for myself, it declared the same truth. One day I hope to spread the love of Christ, to all of those who suffered strife from churches, and the lies they spoke against God for their judgments.

My poetry has never put me in a box and it never will. I have been seen as a Christian poet, and I have yet to accept the title, although I am a Christian, with an anointing for writing. I embody multiple perspectives, that enable myself to encounter people ahead of me, with no intention of being limited to just one group, or type of person. My poems have given me the freedom of explosion; through vocabulary, no one can diminish. I know that I was created for this, and I choose to let God have his way, and I will follow where he sees fit to lead me. My journey for the divine is forever new. His will for me is what I desire to be.

Through every obstacle and tribulation, we reveal the keys to our survival and blessings of all kinds. Mine is defined by nine words of inspiration; strength, perseverance, peace, hope, love, relationships, praise, patience, and prayer. I believe these are the attributes that became relevant to the circumstances I faced, to sustain endurance for this tiring race. Today they are the answers to, what I know to be sure.

I recently finished the book "What I Know For Sure," by Oprah Winfrey that helped me discover the numerous parallels through pain, that my life too, can be a testimony to the world for the opening of doors into purpose. God wanted me to take away the divine *wisdom, from this first half of living, and I thank God every day, for the people who live out there purpose, for me to find mine. From Evangelist Joyce Rodgers and LaTrice Ryan, to Sarah Jakes Roberts, and her husband Toure' Roberts, with the addition of Pastor Keion Henderson, Dr. Myles Monroe, and Apostle Matthew Stevenson. It is a true blessing in knowing the God I serve will lift people, to draw me closer to him.*

When I took the time to analyze what I was experiencing on my journey, I came to realize how signs are everywhere, which allowed me to see that God is always speaking.

I remember when the rapper Dee-1 said, "You have to find your slingshot, to slay your Goliath." We all have a giant in our story to slay, which proves we are victorious.

My slingshot is writing, and my Goliath exists within a variety of barriers that society sets before me. Praise God; my words have versatility. I like to think of it as destiny, finally drawing me near to thee. I am soaring! That's what T. D Jakes taught me, so now it is time I surrender all thoughts to the Lord and pray each day, someone is changed by the words I say.

PART I

Disappointment

How do you get through disappointments?

There is no perfect, or let alone an easy way to overcome disappointment. Every person in this world will have a journey that is so personal, and so unique that no single blueprint can fulfill the details of your life's perspective. I can honestly say that many people can push through any circumstance if they have the right answers, and the will within themselves to put their plans into motion. Disappointments will generally never make you feel good, and I don't believe they are supposed to. When we pay attention to the result of our disappointment, we eventually come to the realization that it worked for our benefit. Not all disappointment comes to bring pain, or discouragement to the spirit, but it positions us towards the direction we ought to go.

In this world, there will be plenty of things we don't understand and many obstacles that will cause us to question what lies ahead. As those moments come, it is our job to seek after God for direction. Although there are people with no faith in a higher power, we all are created by the same God, and he has a plan for us all. Our Father in Heaven has no desire to keep us bound by the disappointments that arise, but to draw us closer to him with redirection in mind. All of our help is found in the highest God, and because his love is everlasting, we can accept his promises of abundance.

Through obedience our disappointments are limited. Knowing that God is for us, he will lead you in the way you are to go, with every opportunity of hope to gain.

CHAPTER 1

Strength

It takes strength...

It takes strength to fight disappointment. Having the quality and state of being physically active is only one portion, but the ability to resist being moved or broken by force is another. We all have the strength inside of us that allows for someone to deal with problems in a determined and effective way. No person is incapable of achieving greatness when they understand the power of resisting attacks. We are human beings, but we are also spirits that are all made in the image of God. The Lord equipped us with everything we need to build ourselves from the inside out, and in doing so, we learn our weaknesses, along with our strengths. I was taught that we live by the spirit and we walk in the flesh, which means we exist amongst two worlds, the natural and the spiritual.

In our natural body, we know that eating healthy and exercising builds our physical strength. In the spirit, we feed on the word of God, which prepares us to war against the enemy of this world we cannot see. Our knowledge of legal, logical, and moral toughness prompts us to be an attribute or fixed asset for the destiny we seek to find, on this spiritual journey. The devil already sees you as a threat, whether we take notice of him, or not. When we activate our degree of potency of effect in the natural, and spirit realm, the concentration is made evident, making room for your intensity of light, color, and sound to permeate the universe with vigor expression.

Encourage yourself...

Our ability to exert effort for the accomplishment of a task lies within our own mind. The energy we need to succeed is waiting to be manifested for the potential to be used as an influence of firepower, for the work of God. When we know what we are capable of there will be no reason to doubt, or worry about the unknown. We give glory and honor to the true and living God that fights for us, but we are made in his image to take heed of our divine qualities, that allow us to pursue and subdue whatever enemies await our present, and future.

To encourage yourself is to believe in your ability to withstand puissance and stress without being distorted, dislodged, or damaged knowing God has empowered you to win every battle. It is essential to stand dependable on the dreams in your heart, as it offers a structure that holds up a foundation for your pursuit in this life. Trust in the process of your plans, when you commit to all you do. And if, disappointment surfaces understand that better is waiting in a different form or direction. Just keep pressing forward in high expectations, and watch time reveal what you are purposed for in its entirety.

"Regardless of Pain"

If we are created in God's image,
Then we are all, beautifully made.

Regardless of the pain and damage,
God provides and comes to our aid.

Do not allow the trauma of the past,
To keep you from, the joy of today.

Some situations were not meant to last,
Thus, God protected you by taking it away.

Give your trust to your heavenly Father,
Let go of what was, or could be in your head.

And watch Jesus take you much further,
Giving you life, more abundantly instead.

"Strength for Dreams"

You can do all things through Christ.
There should be nothing that limits you.
Knowing your strength was in His sacrifice.
He rose so you could have what you pursue.
Today remember the dreams and visions.
The things that fuel your passions to live.
Make a list of plans for your future decisions.
And the course to walk our Father will give
It's never too late to reach a goal.
Don't concentrate on time, do it now.
Everything will work out with God in control.
Just believe and let the Lord figure out how.

"Better is Waiting"

Encouraging yourself in the Lord is not your reaction
in all situations, especially when your heart is massive,
and doubt overpowers meditation. You must fight back
disappointment while using praise as a weapon of inspiration,
for the moments God seems like he's not a blessing.
Outstretched trees will never have to send worship higher
than me! Water filled waves could never sway as swiftly in
dance when I have the chance to flow in the atmosphere
of the Holy Spirit! Why should rocks cry out, when my
mouth is a consuming fire that can never lose its shout.
People, we are to be a grateful nation amid tribulations! Don't
let Satan have the power God has given you when he was
forsaken for blasphemy, and like a tragedy, death is awaiting
those who miss the foreshadowing of the Savior's coming.
Only the strong will survive, the bottom line. It's only a matter
of time, exercise your patience for God's will and your life to
align, and no longer be confined to the things of this world.
Remember his word is accurate, better is waiting for you.

"Profit in Tribulations"

Everyone in this life will make a mistake,
It is how we learn what is wrong from right.
Thank God, His love promises not to forsake,
But takes our darkness and make it bright.

God can turn your flaws into your strength,
To help someone who is struggling too.
Regardless of the issue or time length,
Your tribulations are meant to guide you.

Everything happens for a specific reason,
Either the Lord lead us, or we chose it.
Holy Is our God to protect us from the legion,
And in time His plans for you will profit.

"Soul Power"

If I could take the time to define "soul," I would explain it as the pain, behind every smile that doesn't mind being the stain, that is revealed when you hear or see me…

The soul is the rhythm that convinced the heart to believe it could change its own beat. I could describe it as the illustration of frustration in its calming state of expression…

Am I confusing you?

Maybe because my soul has no purpose in being seen from your point of view…
The soul is more than power or personification of what makes me or another black…

I take that back.

It is my valued redemption of struggles shown as strength. I will forever exemplify all that defies the odds as a minority, I refuse to live less than free…

Let your soul soar in the face of adversity. You are more than your circumstance, and when you know for yourself, you will genuinely advance.

"Better than, Best"

I'm thinking better than, best…

It's my living addressed.
I'm no longer depressed.
There's no settling for less.
My debt is erased.
Nothing is taking my praise.
I'm filled with laughter each day.
Nothing better to say.

I'm living better than, best…
I'm living better than, best.
Since I gave Jesus my yes.
My better is blessed.

What could be better than the best?

Except better.
And yes…
I'm better.

God in Christ...It is our strength.

As amongst most people, we know that strength comes in numbers. The alliances of God with a man makes us unstoppable. Furthermore, we are being regarded as embodying and affording to be supported to conquer, all that provokes the kingdom of God. If God before us, who dare to go against? When we are allowing Christ's firmness of strength to be our maintenance for the rising tendencies of evil. The word of God speaks that we can do all things through Christ that strengthens us; therefore we are only limited in ourselves and not God.

With the strength that materializes from belief in the only begotten son Jesus, that came from Heaven to die and rise from the dead, we are made forceful and productive in the earth. The value of our lives is increased, like a muscle we can tolerate the weights of strain, hardship, and exposure to dangers. Relying on the blood that cleanses our sins, we as believers can now be overcomers of anything, knowing that Christ paid it all. Continuing on this journey, you are set free to change the dynamics of what is wrong in your current circumstance, by trusting in the will of God to empower you like he did Jesus.

To advance beyond any disappointment, we must have a made up mind that God is our source of security. Through discerning power, we can see how he operates in us, as well as in others to be a blessing. His plans are not to harm us, but to bring us into a life of prosperity for his namesake. That his name will be glorified in the earth, and for his children to be well off for eternity, covering the multitudes with his love so that he can save us all from the foul intentions of Satan. Let the confessions of your heart unto God provide you with the answers for your life disappointments, as he releases the truth into your soul for comfort in prevailing.

CHAPTER 2

Perseverance

I have to persevere…

I have to persevere to get through my disappointments on this journey of life. Like strength, perseverance is required to survive when you don't know what to do, or where to go. It is for us to continue doing something, or at least keep trying, to do anything even though it is difficult. Persisting at every state against various enterprises or undertakings, in spite of counter influences, opposition, and discouragement. For in our striving we are always growing closer to revelations, whether we agree with the results of our choices, or not. Working your natural and spiritual qualities, to awaken the opportunities predestined beyond the imaginations, we embark upon serenity.

Through continuous efforts, or actions, and belief in God, you can achieve something despite difficulties, failures, or finances because of the conditions of your heart. When you are upright with the Lord in your heart, he will see to it that everything will work out for you. Perseverance is the test to perfect your skills for the task you choose to focus upon. In this world, we cannot make excuses, but we are to persist in the speech of our tongue, through interrogation, arguments, and hatred from those who do not believe in what you do. No battle is given to the swift, but to those who endure the trials and tribulations with joy to win.

Don't Quit.

In true inspiration, it's only right to know that you should never quit. The best things in life are not offered freely in my opinion, simply because anything you desire comes with determination. The highest level of achievement varies from person to person, but generally, the same efforts can be measured equally across different categories. It takes hard work, motivation, inspiration, and dedication to get up and move every day, believing that you will achieve your dreams. Not everyone carries those characteristics naturally, but they do exist in us spiritually.

It is for us to understand and learn who we are through our disappointments. God uses these moments in our lives to give us reflections of ourselves. Only the Lord knows what is on the other side. However, he gives us dreams to keep reminding us what's to gain when you push.

Let your trust in God take you to the heights you need to reach in this world because we are not promised every day, but we can still get purpose from each one. When we quit, we tell the devil he wins. As children of God, we do not fail to the hands of the enemy. Failure is just another way for you to regain focus on the task, or to try something new. Failure should never be accepted in the heart of anyone, knowing that it can paralyze and mute you. Many people are walking the earth hardened by their life circumstances and others that are paralyzed by traumas. These people are those that have fallen asleep, moving in the realms of their thoughts with no footprints on the earth.

We fail when we do not bear fruit of our best in each new season. Repeating cycles of generational curses, we fail to change. Don't let your disappointments keep you in the bondage of your own slavery when Christ has already come to set you free. Our disappointments are never to keep us from fulfilling a lifelong paradise with our heavenly Father. Let perseverance take you to no limits, by shouting, running, and planning so that the world can see the change it needs with your gifts from above, that only the creator can give.

"Growing Pains"

Things in life don't always work out,
Sometimes it's for the right reason.
Not meant to make you give up, or doubt,
Yet show you what's a part of your season.

Some things in life are destined to change,
That's the reality of knowing you are growing.
Accepting God's plan for yours in exchange,
It's a success no matter where you are going.

All things work for the good of those,
Who loves the Lord according to his purpose.
If we live right with nothing hidden to expose,
His love for us will show itself to be luscious.

"Transition Time"

Winter is gone, and spring has arrived,
Exiting another season you have survived.

Rejoice in gladness for your trials to come,
Showing the enemy where your help came from.

God wants to reveal intentions for your year,
Expecting you to seek him so you may hear,
What is the truth as the end draws near?
To keep you covered from the spirit of fear.

This world and its sin will soon pass away,
It's now time to humble ourselves and pray.

We must turn from our ways to live saved,
Or travel the road to hell Satan already paved.

"Chance to Advance"

It's a new week for you to advance,
To rear ambiguity and take a chance,
Forgetting what is behind at a glance,
To be the example Christ can enhance.

You have nothing to lose in God's hand,
He will do whatever to help you stand,
As he guides you throughout the land,
Showing you that life with him is grand.

We should strive harder to reach dreams,
Merging together like waters in streams,
For us to be more potent as teams,
And put an end to the devil's schemes.

"Creative Believer"

At what point will double standards take the back road?

I was never told in my Bible that a believer,

Is unable to use the name of Christ,

To encourage the population through,

Any artistic form of verbal expression.

Be ye set apart…

Be ye clean…

Be ye holy…

If these teachings remain the same...

Why then are Christians to blame for their skill?

Accepting the reward of talent as a part of God's will,

For us to bring up a nation of followers who,

Rap, sing, dance, act, and write poetry.

…Or whoever else they

Want to be…

This world can be so hypocritical and mean.

The church says it's too worldly...

The world says it's too preachy…

So, where does the creative believer dwell?

When God is telling them… Don't quit.

"Pressing Through Storms"

I sometimes struggle to understand the path to take...

Every day I wake I make the decision to seek

A higher power to lead me in the direction

I was created to walk...

I continue to press each day toward a better life

Often seen in dreams

And in between the hardships of living

I pay the price sown in tears...

Yet never will I fear the future ahead of me...

Instead, I search for my joy often hidden

By the low clouds that form during my storm...

Thankfully the fighter in me keeps growing stronger daily.

"A Believer's Battle"

It's not as simple as I thought, being a believer,
Many moments I want to fulfill my own desires,
Without looking like the few Christian deceivers,
I strive to be someone who transparently inspires.

We are not perfect, but don't use excuses for sin,
When slips are steps to where we should begin,
From betrayal, addiction, depression, and sorrow,
These are the things that end someone's tomorrow.

If God forgives us, why not exemplify his love as well,
It's challenging to live righteously religiously continuously,
While the truth is camouflaged behind white lies we tell,
Now is the time to resemble what we've learned spiritually.

"Belief Beyond Disappointment"

Disappointments are necessary adjustments when the heart, and mind have illustrated the full outcome that should be projected... Causing faith to be no light task when your hope is focused on the things you ask, and not in whom you trust and believe...

God has a plan that can outshine every time we
ever felt like giving up if we press forward by
forgetting what is behind and looking up...
We must remember all our ideas are not on the
same level as His, for the thoughts he thinks
towards us are higher than we were taught...
Yet and still His will shall never return void, to those
who embody the truth in all that we go through...

His promises are yes and amen, but this is not for every man that delights in worldly ventures, however to those who submit themselves to his written scriptures to obtain their desires...
God wants to take us higher, to abstain his children
from a consuming fire in hell, if we let go of the
sexual mentality that locks the shell...
Simply put you must know He's real to open up the senses to feel his presence and comprehend the real purpose of all intentions.

Believe you can succeed...

Many people are on their journey of life with little direction in which they are to go or believe they have no way out. The power of belief should never be underestimated, for it is the source of what drives us as human beings. Our very belief system determines how the world is illustrated today. When we do not have a strong belief in ourselves, we eliminate our purpose of living. The brain is programmed to keep us on track towards a destiny, yet if we do not fill it with the right nutrition it needs for success, it will not prosper. We are blessed to have mouths that can speak words that even we can believe. The more we feed our minds with aspirations and goals, we then can train the rest of the body to follow.

Let go of the negativity that the world tries to use against your success, by turning it into the very energy that can propel you forward. The enemies of the world are the enemies of God, and what God has for you will never be stopped, by the control of any man he created. No person has the power to limit your growth towards success, except you. We are to become partners with God and fight the battles of this universe with him in the front. When God is with you, you can definitely believe in your success! It's a yes, and Amen! Tell yourself, that disappointments will not limit your progress, and that believing in God, you will be successful in all things. By faith when you think about it, you can most certainly receive it.

"You Will Win"

More often you should praise God before avoiding askance...
Knowing your desires and needs will fall in your hands...
Life is going to always come with high demands...
Affirm your release of peace amid the circumstance...
You will allow God's presence to appear in a trance...
There are points in which you must understand...
Obedience is a requirement to obtain your abundant inheritance...

Trust in the Lord with all your heart and never...
Depart from His teachings, fear not the evils of this world...
For His love continue reaching...
Jesus is waiting for your undeniable faith, to bless...
You in your latter day. Keep giving him glory...
No matter the plot within your story...

He is the author and finisher.
The Alpha and Omega.
He knows your beginning and end.
So, know that with him...
You will win.

"It's Turning Around"

I will bless the Lord at all times
No matter how hard the tribulations
Even when I don't have a dime
His love is my undying inspiration
I will forget what is over and gone
Pressing forward through each day
Knowing that with Christ I'm not alone
I can trust in every word he say
Don't let the enemy get you down
Hold your head up and stand your ground
Smile continuously don't ever frown
When God knows it's turning around

"Prospering Purpose"

If God said he's going to do it, believe him,

He is not a man that should lie,

His promises are too legit, so no need to quit,

When he said, he will fix it.

If leaning on your own understanding,

Conflicts with your trust, then you must find,

A praise buried in the dust, even if you feel deserted,

No dry place can hinder the well that forever spills.

Your worship is a lifestyle, not only offered up,

Be convinced of yourself, don't allow doubt,

To count you out when God has designed,

A prosperous path for you to rise and shine.

We must let go of an imaginary faith with no disappointments,

Suffering is apart of the purpose to keep you focused on Him,

He desires to become one with you, and in the process, bless you too,

Like any relationship, it won't be all about you.

He deserves love and adoration too,

Seek Him daily and hopefully more than once to hear,

His voice because in this world, to live joyful,

God is the best choice.

"Let God Lead"

I think in various magnitudes,
So far in depth, I feel the debts of those who,
Lose control of life contingencies.
It's no coincidence my poetry can align with the hostility,
And reconnect with the spirituality hidden within thee.
The Holy Spirit has a way of advocating on your behalf,
While others laugh, He has the last.
Intently acquainting to what you repeat,
Grasp Heaven's peak in which we seek, letting no,
Moment of release be silenced, when we have voices to speak.
Let defiance break its curse from birth by pursuing its worth in glory,
Now is not the time to subject to traditions of slavery,
When nothing is overcome without bravery.
No empty seed, nor filthy greed can cause you to succeed,
If God in all is not who leads.
He is just, kind, and everything we're hoping to find,
Bringing pure joy with peace,
To ignite zeal that never ceases.

"Doubt, Fear & Worry"

Doubt…
Fear...
Worry...

It all ends here.

No longer will these things of the past provoke my intuition to become paralyzed to my own demise…
I choose today to rise into new measures of my purpose like the wise
I will give God the praise with both hands raised…
Fazed…I won't be. I press forward towards destiny. I await the plan my Father has for me...
Permanently will worship drip from my lips to quench my thirst for more of you oh God!
Forever will I hide the bribes of depression that tries to supply frustration during my patience in waiting for you!
The future is brighter for every fighter striving to go higher, may the desire of your heart manifest until your day of rest, with much love, perseverance, and happiness. In all your doings…

be blessed.

"Understanding Disappointment"

Life is full of so many ups and downs
Yet there is still much to be discovered.
Before we receive our heavenly crowns
There are things here we need recovered.
God has more tests in this walk to come
Many you'll repeat if they go unlearned.
Subjecting to burdens you already succumb
Thankfully His grace is our gift returned.
Use disappointment as a guiding light
Seeking the revelations beyond the flesh.
Thus, allowing the inner spirit to ignite
As we open ourselves for God to refresh.

"Living Free"

I believe in chances…
The advances that come in life for you to take,
Your place in destiny.
I believe in love…
The glove that secures the purity of my heart,
From the mess of sin.

Yet I am searching…
For my inner power to manifest within every,
Given hour.
Yet I am starving…
For my inner wisdom to profess the secrets of,
My kingdom come.

I'm living for more than right now, a somehow…
I'll make it …don't worry, I'll fake it… mentality.
God has granted more to me than promised to be…
That's why I lift my hands to thee…no more
Complaining when…He has spoken…
You're free.

PART II

Hardship

Why do bad things happen to good people?

I've come to the understanding that hardship is inevitable in this world. Not that it's always fair to the person who experiences the suffering, but it all serves a purpose when we make our pain prosperous. The fact that we are all created with free will allows for a variety of choices and possibilities to unfold when relating to good and evil. Some people are raised to treat others with love and kindness, and yet those same children grow to make decisions that can be passed on, or they can choose to rebel against their teachings. And in another home children can be abused, or even neglected by their parents, but those persons can develop alternative thinking by choosing to treat others the opposite way they were treated, knowing that it hurt them, and they would instead not pass on those same feelings they endured.

We cannot control the lives of anyone but our own, and with our personal experience, we still have to answer to God, unless we decide to deny him of his existence. There are many reasons as to why bad things happen, we can turn on the news or get on social media and see all of the negativity that is produced from the poor judgment of human beings. As we see the results of their thinking, we are generally left to wonder, why, but the truth of the matter is that we are accountable for how we impact the life of another. No person does wrong for all the same reasons. Some happen by accident, others from hateful and cruel intentions, where for some it is in their perspective of survival.

Bad times may come in different appearances, and they are generally due to the systems of this world that promote the demise of another to overcome. When we continue to sow seeds of jealousy, envy, and thieving it is not hard to realize how the world reached its present state. People have been suffering for centuries from the same problems, and mainly from the thirst of power, or the idea of being on top in whatever you do. Cheating, scamming, and lying is buried in the DNA of many bloodlines with no comprehension of change. One day perhaps, the intellect of generations to come can reverse the curse of hatred, by focusing on the positivity we can bring when we value the life of another.

CHAPTER 3

Patience

I have to be patient...

I have to be patient during hardships to see what the ends are going to be. I believe in the impossible, and I know that greatness is not going to come overnight, nor will it come in any quick pace we truly desire it to arrive. Our most enormous cravings in life are birthed overtime. Passion doesn't even develop instantaneously, most people realize their love for something the longer they are involved with it. Whether it be another person, a job, an instrument, a sport, an art form, or any other passion one can imagine. The point is most people further their passion when they hold on to whatever it is they connect to, and only patience can reveal what's concealed inside.

We all are capable of being able to remain calm, and not become annoyed when waiting for long moments in time. Making note that when dealing with problems, or difficult people there will always be an opportunity for you to prove you have self-control, and to exercise your discipline. The flesh is an untamed vessel in its natural state, which has to be disciplined. Investing efforts of time for the shaping of your mind and heart, to find what not only makes you tick with anger but what you have to live for. We are all fighting a war more significant than ourselves, whether we accept it, or not.

When we increase our patience, we discover what lies beneath our passions and gifts, which is to take us forward in God.

True intentions are displayed in a particular way over a long period, with no need of worrying. Some people will forever jump to conclusions with no efforts to wait, as others will open the window of time to reach clarity. As with God, his patience with us shows his genuine love for us. Being the creator of all things in the universe and the heavens, God wants us to obtain the best he can give his children. Through faith, we know that patience prepares the pathway for destiny. There is no need to rush for anything, use wisdom to analyze the prize that is waiting on the other side. Remember that anxiety is a reflection of your patience for the road you are on. No need to be hasty, answers are usually replied when we take the time to receive them. We can lighten our mental loads when we rest and choose to shift perspectives, believing better is still there awaiting our arrival.

"Patience During Disappointment"

Life is not what you always expect,
It's full of disappointments and stress.
But your problems God will not neglect,
Taking His time to remove all your mess.
Commit all of your works unto the Lord,
And your ideas in time He will establish.
Remember there's nothing God can't afford,
When your sins are abandoned for demolish.
Let these coming days be a chance to reflect,
Don't wait until Sunday to request restoration.
Tomorrow isn't promised let's live to be direct,
With patients at the source of a new revelation.

"Awaiting Love"

In this world today, we don't enjoy the wait.

Yet through worldly customs, we compensate,
While ignoring the plans God orchestrate,
That will one day lead us to our soul mate.

Do you ever consider why we truly date?

Or why marriages start well then desolate,
Because singleness isn't taught to celebrate,
But teaching generations how to procreate.

Being single is nothing you should ever hate.

It reveals what's in your life to concentrate,
When you connect with God, you graduate,
Making you whole, then love he incorporate.

"Lustful Temptation"

What is it about lust that leads us to sin?
Temptation as the influence it reveals the truth,
By exciting what you desire most within,
As seduction screams your name so uncouth.

Lust comes in the form of materials and sex,
Contributing to more than one type of hex,
You must understand that it's deeply complex,
To give into emotions that can leave your tomorrow vex.

How does one take control of passion?
That burns inside for the wrong reasons,
When what is bad feels really good in action,
But understand to God it's still treasons.

"Undeniable Faith"

Many wonder how the God I serve came to be,
I tell them he always existed, He is an eternity.

They may not believe it because it wasn't recorded,
But those thoughts for me were long aborted.

Who wrote the Bible? How do we know they're real?
I tell them it takes an open mind to feel.

Faith is your key to the reality of His presence,
Seeing isn't always believing for God's essence.

Can you dare to fathom a God you can't touch?
For me, it isn't always easy, but he is my crutch.

When I can't explain anymore, I just start to pray,
No need to force it the Lord is able, He is the way.

"Questionable Faith"

There are some moments, my faith is questionable,
Because I have days of disarray, that is unstable.

Sometimes I look to the hills, but my help still waits,
My clock of salvation expiring, patience as its traits.

Answered prayers are unnoticed when doubt arise,
But if praise and rejoicing, are what's being raised,

There should be no surprise, it's coming with no lies,
Only if you believe, then you receive to be amazed.

Being saved isn't easy when you can't surrender all,
Yet we commit to worldly things, both big and small.

Perhaps the truth will come to be, setting you free,
So that we will indeed grow, leading to prosperity.

"It's a New Season"

It's a new season, and it's a brighter day!
A fresh anointing is flowing your way!
A season of power and prosperity,
For those that are called, and choose to believe,
The greater you seek, is already here to receive,
You've soiled the seed, through faith and tears,
Rejoice in His goodness with no doubt or fears.

No prayer has gone unheard, but there were delays,
Of long-suffering that had them deferred,
To prepare you for the blessing you rightfully deserve,
Although not preferred, God requires patience,
And praise that proves you are worthy of,
The request you raise.

Be encouraged for the best, is still yet to come,
With expectancy as your urgency, be persistent,
And worship in the face of the Lord honoring,
His majesty and await the true magnificent glory.

How long do I have to wait...

The older I get, the more I see the benefit in my waiting. With so much to gain in this world, no one does it by just hoping. Every dream is a vision until you make it a goal, from a goal it becomes a plan, and once you make a plan, it is on you to pursue.

Preparation is proof of maturity, exemplifying the well thought out perceptions that details take time. There will be some things in our lives that will come faster than others, but the best is built in milestones. We can expect the great at a projected point in our lives, but when hardship strikes it can set us back. When these moments arrive, it is the right time to test how patient you are.

A person knows they exercise steadfast patience when they can bear pains or trials calmly without complaint. It may take years to achieve, but soon you will see manifesting forbearance under provocation that used to cause you strain. Becoming more steadfast despite any opposition, disrespect, or adversity that may offer to offend your presence. Then healing can take place in the areas of your life, that will prepare you for better days. There is no one person, who has walked this earth, that has not experienced hardship. Therefore we all know some type of pain, making it more essential for us to heal. In waiting, we are prepared to focus on the imperfections that hold us back from purpose. When we get to the root of our problems we flourish in the place of our callings. Through the healing of our hardships, we are made known to the wholeness needed to help others.

"Awaiting the Miracle"

I can admit that I put my hope, and trust in the,
Invisible to receive my miracles,
I've waited for years, and shed so many tears for,
Things that have yet to appear, but faith didn't,
Promise me blessings instantaneously.
Patience is a virtue, I've learned to understand,
Because with God in full control he requires,
Waiting as a high demand, so I just keep on,
Praising him as long as I can.
He knows the desires of your heart, he is the one,
Who created them from the very start by,
Knowing your ending, before your beginning.
There is a reason for every want in your life,
Whether it brings you joy or heartache it is all,
Geared to rear you closer to destiny if you,
Don't allow setbacks, to be your primary focus,
When a comeback, is a part of the purpose.
Things won't be perfect all the time when,
Too many people exist, with free will in your reality,
But, thankfully he promised you better if you,
Would just let go, and let him lead you to where,
You ought to be.

"Writer's Block…"

I haven't had much to say lately…
Today seems the same way…
Reaching for more than simple rhymes to…
Entice the mind about hopes for the present…
Times that the past can no longer bind…

I struggled to move my hands to produce…
My thoughts giving me writer's block…

Stocks of knowledge and wisdom demanding…
From me freedom to roam for new homes to…
Implant seeds for those who need encouraging…

Uncertain of things to come I wait for words to…
Form that could transform my meaning into purpose…
Sometimes it takes more effort to focus…
When life has no details of what it prevails to…
Expose in the path of those who seek more…
Than right now…

Yet somehow smiles have to abound…
But thankfully when you read between…
Lines eventually meaning can be found…

"Ability to Wait"

I believed that if I put my...
Trust in God it would take the pain away,
But at times it increased...
Praying the pain would cease,
He said it would decrease my praise...
My latter days have yet, to raise into pillars...

From on high,
The nights I cried have not watered all of...
My seeds that were sown to reap,
Maybe they haven't grown because of my...
Inability to wait joyfully...

My blessings are beyond the knowledge of man...
And what God has planned, can only be greater,
Than the hell I face in this place...
So this time my tears, won't erupt from fear of,
Doubting its timely arrival...
I'll just keep reading my Bible, and searching,
For my direction to follow...
And keep faith in my heart from the past,
I can forever borrow...

"Sacrificing Power"

I've learned the power of sacrifice and its ability
To free from the natures of sin
Fasting helped me alleviate while passing
Through this world's lies and to my surprise I
Was able to elevate spiritually
Grow with wisdom mentally
Control my lacking emotionally
While catering to my temple physically
See I know the waring of spirituality and its
Tendency to shed light on the fight I face in the
Midst of the space in my mind
The things that hold me blind to the truths of
My youth and suppresses the growth of my soul
My Father helped me gain control over the things
That kept me bound so that I could no longer surround myself
With the temptations that contradict what I'm told
But the presence of the enemy is so bold
Jesus, my Lord
Holy spirit my way maker
We need you more than prayers are prayed
Not wanting to end up dead but we cry out
In the silence instead dreading the guilt and fear
Of internal pasts, the devil reminds of these things to
Cut our blessings in half as habits of rebellion
Oppresses millions from a relationship with an
Eternal loving God

His rod and staff comfort us but if Satan

Can get you to deny your trust in the Lord

Through the betrayal of the word as the

Facade of race and the absence of unity

Then people really don't know how much of heaven

For themselves, they're ruining

"Rules of Waiting"

Waiting isn't easy...
When dating is the proper ideal for mating...

Waiting isn't fair...
When imitating is your habit that's,
Circulating.

Waiting isn't right...
When isolating is required for your,
Meditating.

Waiting is not what we teach yet what we,
Falsely preach...
A shame to most and the fame for those who
Find no blame in promiscuous games.

Waiting is not for the week at heart, who quit,
Whatever they start...
The pretenders who become lenders before,
Borrowers until you surrender to the mender.

Waiting is for the broken to heal, the dreamer,
To expand, the musicians to sing, the prophet to
Listen, the leader to rise...to counter our demise...
There's much more to waiting...than rules of dating.

"Hours with God"

I spent time with God for hours…

I wanted to know what it was like to seek his face and,
Witness His great power.

I heard him speak to me for hours…

I listened to him tell me stories of the past and His,
Plans for sin to, scour.

I fasted for several days…and hours…

I endured long suffering to condition my desire to,
Persevere over what devours.

I trusted for countless hours…

I failed to touch the tangible dreams I had instantly,
Seen of yours, and ours.

I never stopped no matter the hour…

I stayed faithful to God for manifestations of his will,
To heal so, today blessings could shower.

CHAPTER 4

Praise

I have to praise my way through...

Praising is my life release for peace. I learned how to press through hardships by giving my heart to God. Growing up in church I witnessed the praising of God through the older saints, and honestly, it was my favorite part. I loved watching my Great Grandma give God her all, to hear her lift up shouts of triumph, and joy to her savior. To see the tears that would continuously well in the eyes of God's children and the uncontrollable nature of behaviors.

Not all praise takes the same form, mainly because praise is a reaction of the spirit, as well as the conscious choice to gratify the name of the Lord. You do not have to be overtaken by a ghost to honor the presence of an honorable King. Our praise is an oath unto the creator who made us as a gift to himself. The very breath we breathe is praise unto the ears of our Father, we owe him our lives.

Let us say good things about the God of all creation, expressing our approval of his perfect plans. Thanking him for his love with respect for his glory. Lifting up words of how great the qualities of

God is, he is worthy to be exalted in all the earth. I will bless the Lord at all times, for he has brought me through the hardships of this world with a humble heart. God never let me go, and he will never let you go. God will forever be the protection in this world we need whenever we fall.

"A Birth Praise"

There isn't enough vocabulary to bless you,
Your presence is like the water to my soul.
Never can I live without a drink or two,
As you fill me daily and I'm made whole.
I'm nothing more than what you made of me,
Awaiting my destiny, I bow down to my knee.
With mercy and grace, you count me worthy,
And with praise in my heart, I give to thee.
To you, I give the glory and honor in all ways,
Shouting and dancing for your gift of birth.
I will spread your gospel throughout my days,
Until the day you call me to leave this earth.

"Daily Worship"

A journey I had no choice in
This path for me was chosen and yet so
Much gratitude flows from the depths of
My heart to worship you
God there is no purpose or fulfillment for life
If your son did not pay the price
I'm in awe of your grace and mercy
Not only towards me but your people
We don't deserve your blessings but
Because of your patience we learn
The lessons to achieve who you
Want us to be
God with all I am I give myself daily
Continue to use me for your glory
I pray that you get the praise from your
Children through my works
Let the abundance of cries be released
From every mouth
Let every flesh die before you
And let every spirit man do as you plan
You are an awesome God
Let your name be exalted above all

"Believing God's Greatness"

Waking up to you is nothing less than the sunlight...

Perfect beam in the daybreak of summer...

Your touch is the purest form of intimacy...

I breathe off of the very air you breathe into me...

Daily I reverence your presence...

Like the very water, I embody I can't be without you...

Jesus your like instruments to a beat...

The shout within my feet...

The praise in my hand raise...

The worship to the lips and tongue...

That can never go undone...

I marvel at your grace towards me...

Your love is the ultimate seducer drawing me...

Closer with your perfection of truth and trust...

There's no one greater than you...

Mountain's can't imitate your greatness in height...

Or altitudes...space can't fill in the area to your...

Minds beginning and end...

Fire has no temperature to compare to the passion...

You feel for your creation...

No earthquake can shake up the enemy's camp...

In the lives of your people like you can...

I stand in awe of you...I just wish that one day...

The unbelievers can have the same feelings For you...

That I do.

"Falling in God's Will"

The Lord is a mighty strong tower,
He makes things right, when I choose to sin,
There will never be a time when I won't call,
Out Jesus name, and praise.
Father with my hands up,
Let you see, the sincerity in me.

Lord, it's hard, doing your will,
When the life for you I live, the devil wants to kill,
Forever disguising himself, in someone new,
I always have to pray, to find out who.

I'm your soldier...
Your little shepherd...
No other master, shall I have before thee,
Give me clarity, as I continue to carry this cross,
To never stay down when I fall, like the enemy.
With my head looking up, you will be the one to
Carry me, as I rest in your arms so comfortably.

"Spiritual Belief"

I believe in miracles.
The supernatural things, very few can truly understand.
I believe in prayers.
The power of words going up, and the laying of hands.
I believe in spiritual tongues.
The language which others, can't verbally comprehend.

Like my Father as three in one...
Father, Holy Spirit, and son...
He is my Alpha and Omega...
My beginning and end...
Who forgives me of every sin...
The King of kings...
And creator who rules all things...

He is the great "I Am" that covers me and does,
Not condemn out of His love for me,
He freed me...took me back, and cradled me,
Told me...no more lack...

Thank you, Lord, for dying, on Calvary so that I could,
Be able to make the mistakes, and be forgiven,
To be who you called me to be,
So I could say again...Devil, I'm free!

Open your mouth...

One of the biggest mistakes we make as human beings is choosing to quiet ourselves. There is a right time to hush, and then there are signs of maturity in which you discern when to respond accordingly. The enemy wants to keep us censored and silent, sensing us as a threat, he understands that our mouth is a powerful weapon. We can speak life into existence, from the thoughts of our mind, to shape the world. As hardships surround your lives lift up the praises God inhabits, and watch the situations in your life begin to change. Calling on the name of Jesus, he will see to it that the Father will answer you.

Open your mouth with thanksgiving, spreading love to the true and living God.

Arousing the heavens, he will send angels on your behalf. Sing, dance, and play instruments with sincerity as the weights of the world are placed in the hands of a mighty God. The Lord is magnificent in all his ways! Hallelujah! His dominion is above any other reign. My God has never lost a battle, and he never will! When we lift up our praise with a loud voice, we give our problems less control, and we accept the yoke of the Holy Spirit. Cleansing us of our transgressions, purging us of our iniquity, we surrender to the sovereignty of your power. The Lord is worthy to be praised.

Trust in the path God leads you, hardships are just enemies to war off with your faith in Jesus. Believing that Christ in you will make you victorious over every situation, keep praise on your tongue. Confusing the devil with your joy in the Lord, remember that your better days are still yet to come. Praise God that he fulfills his promises for all that trust in him. There is no reason to doubt, no obstacle can defeat you. Turn up the praise, and profess the blessings you desire to see! We are the head and not the tail, with God we shall prevail! Amen!

"Lessons Before Blessings"

Hardships are not generally overcome effortlessly...

When you've convinced your heart, of a lie, you didn't see

coming... Hope fallen in the course of tragedy, senseless to feel...

How can people get mad, at others who

can't discern what's fake or real...

Betraying the hearts of strangers, who

appear to be family or friends...

What do you expect me to say as a believer?

That the battle gets more relaxed when you call on Jesus...

At every sign of trouble, and think He won't allow you to struggle...

Your blessings come from the lessons we face daily...

God knows what to use, to bring you towards

a place of an expected end...

But know the test isn't to convict you always...

However to consistently show, the devil

he can't restrict your praise.

"Desiring Praise"

You, God, are my refuge, in the midst of evil spirits,
That seek to devour my flesh. You are the very,
Breath that flows like the wind, carrying me into,
My place of rest, Lord your will is my heart's desire,
Your righteousness abounds in my dreams purifying,
My mind of all kinds of sin.
Father, you mean everything to me, I will worship you,
Forever and for whatever years and days are to come.
Your kingdom will have reign over me,
Jesus your name is excellent,
An all-powerful and mighty sword,
Defeating all my enemies seen and unseen.
You are victorious, any battle you encounter you win,
There is no one above you, I love you, all that I am,
I will give back willingly to you, my spirit cries out in praise
My flesh bows with no distress as my tongue,
Says yes.
Lord make me what you want me to be, use me, Lord,
To do your great works, remove all hurt and shame,
That keeps me from you, God, I turn away from,
Anything not like you! Do what you want to.
Hear me Father and come to my rescue, when enemies
Try to pursue me, I want to grow in you, Give me
More of you, I want more of you, fill me and renew a,
Right spirit unshakeable, and able to serve you.

"Praise for Bad Days"

I've learned that the bad days, can't last always,
Not when you fight back, in the battle with praise.
Although your heart may be heavy, don't let it stay,
Instead look to the Father, with your head upraised.

My mouth is my weapon, in this spiritual warfare,
The Bible is the key, to destroy the devil's territory.
No demon in hell will overcome, we've got the victory.
Let us worship the Lord, in total peace without care.

Disaster may strike, even during some rough times,
But Jesus will fix it, so no need to commit a crime.
Just acknowledge him daily, in the face of trouble,
And he guarantees like for Job, to give you double.

"Life of Worship and Praise"

Worship and praise should be more than temporary,
Expressions but a lifestyle...
God is worthy of honor, and adoration yet many,
Deprive him of reverence until their needs,
Become a menace...
At what point will people magnify the Lord coherently,
Regardless if he delivers them from their enemies...
Jesus has already done more than enough and,
Exaltation of His wondrous name will outpour,
Blessings when things get tough...

Maybe one day the world will want more than His,
Power to work miracles, perhaps if many would edify,
The spiritual they could witness the supernatural...
Christ is not a fable, to suppress the minds of any,
Particular race, but non believers would know this,
If they knew how to seek his face...
Just know that He's coming back with glory to rapture,
Those who stayed on track, when God cracks the sky,
It'll be too late to repent or pray so why wait...
When you can give your life today.

"An Exalted Praise"

This is the day that the Lord has made and I will rejoice and be glad
in it!
My soul shall make a boast in the Lord that deplores,
All things impure in your sight!
Your holiness and righteousness, I will humbly adore!
As I worship you forevermore!
Your heavenly gates, Father is my strongest desire!
Though tried by the fire, like your streets I'll be paved in gold!
With riches untold, I will praise you daily while I wait!
You're mighty to save and impressive in all your ways!
Jesus is what I call you with no hesitation, Hosanna is,
What angels cry out in acclamation!
Sovereign and magnificent, is your majesty!
Royal and omnipotent, is your wondrous glory!
Highly exalted, will you eternally reign!
One second in your presence, no one will ever be the same!
And I will ceaselessly reverence your hallowed name!

"Praise for New Beginnings"

It's a time of new beginning, and my arms are
Opened wide to receive
Releasing anger, selfishness, depression, and pride
The things I don't need
No longer will I hide behind the doors of the past
Knowing in the light darkness cannot last
I'm moving forward towards more fabulous days
No more tears are allowed to stay
Happiness won't come effortless when trials are continuous
But thank God they're not limitless

Heavenly Father, I will forever give you the praise
Hallelujah to you I will eternally raise
Jesus your love I will unfailingly know
The compassion you give strengthens me to grow
Holy spirit how you love me the world has yet even to show
So I'll carry you with me wherever I go
I'm not the same because you called me by name
Displaying how much you thought of me
To one day elevate me for all the world to see
How change through you brought out the best in me

"Professing God's Greatness"

God you are sovereign, your implementation in the heavens...

And the earth is full of your splendor...

No creature in the sea, nor on the land go without...

The directions of your hands...

Everything you do is of perfection in all your...

Miracles, signs, and wonders...

Father of creation we reverence your presence...

For in you are the truths of this world placed in us...

From our youths, to fulfill your plans as man over Satan...

You reign!

You're holy!

You're mighty!

Lord of Lords!

King of Kings!

Nothing measures to the pleasure of an all-knowing God...

As you continue to reveal yourself step by step as we cry out for help...

Your mercy never fails us even when we fail to trust...

But forgiveness covers us...

You are matchless the living and supernatural being that keeps on seeing...

And doing great things for me...

To you, I owe my spirit and flesh, and to you, I will daily profess...

With all that's within me, whatever you ask...

Shall be yes.

"Planted in God"

Words are not always hard to express when compared,
To the life, I live to impress you,
No amount of words used can confuse actions of,
My worship when it comes to praising you,
I marvel in the glory you reveal to me.

Father, my expectations of your power, are not conformed,
Within every changing hour, I patiently wait for the miracles,
Upon your arrival, Jesus your love I will forever seek,
In a distorted land, in hopes to one day dwell in your,
Garden of Eden again.

Planted with your vision in mind, buried with your victory,
To find covered securely with your touch,
Watered with your presence to stand, warmed with your sun,
To one day follow in your son's shadow, Lord I grow only,
Because of you, to show what your beauty in the world is supposed
to do.

I exalt the holy and righteousness of you, never is my desire to be away,
From you my father and creator, my peace and mediator, no edification,
From my mouth to heaven will be thwarted you,
Will complete the work in me you started.

PART III

Loss

With the loss, what have I gained?

The loss of a loved one can never show its positive impact at the given moment. In the sight of God, life never ends. Being that we live amongst two worlds, natural and spiritual, we take in two deaths. When our loved ones pass from this world into another, we are reminded of the truths that life is not promised daily. Whether they pass from natural causes, disease, or murdered we feel the separation of a soul, which we will no longer see going forward each day. In those nights of sorrow, God is watching over you, preparing comfort in the place of your grieving. Jehovah is sovereign, and just to heal the broken-hearted.

Through the unexpected loss of a loved one, I know that there is an answer in God. The Lord is sure to make everything work for our good, not only in material things but in the wellness of life. No one is meant to be sad their whole life when God sent his son Jesus to overcome it all. Everything that we lose we gain in God. We are all created to activate the will of God on the earth. Our time here is meant to be limited through the admission of sin. We are to serve God to find the purpose in which we are to fulfill, as did Christ Jesus. All are purposed through the Father, but it is for us to discipline ourselves in obedience, to receive wisdom.

Loss is temporary when we understand the plans of God. He intends to unite all his children together again in Heaven. When the Lord returns, we will all be made known of the son, and we will bow to worship Jesus. He will come for his people, bringing us before the Father to behold a new home. Our faith is in the heart of God, He loves us so, that he patiently waits for us to get ourselves right.

There is a purpose in every life that passes through the womb of a woman. With our free will we have the power to make conscious choices, that produce reactions in the earth. Jesus death on the cross altered the world for an eternity. And like death, it can modify the existence of our patterns, rupturing our memory tracks. No one cares for change when it's not offered, but demanded upon you. Your routines of life taken from its direction, you are forced to accept the differences to come. It's challenging to ignore drastic shifts, yet in every loss, there is something to be found. My gift of poetry was birthed after the passing of my Great Grandmother at the age of twelve. I knew nothing of loss at that time, in the magnitude it brought to my heart. However, God knew what to do, to release what was on the inside of me.

From my broken heart, the seeds of poetry rose. Watered with my tears, I poured out my soul in the traces of words. My will being revealed in my pain, I had more to gain beyond the grief of my loss. To know that I was anointed to speak into the hearts and minds of people around the world, sharing the love of God through rhythm and rhyme. I planned to expand to new heights, believing that God would make it alright. Like many deaths in the world, we know that very few awaken the minds of people to change. Why wait for more death for the betterment of our families and communities. Allow the Lord to use every life as a sign that he is God, who can guide the trails of your tears towards the path you needed to find. Death is an awakening, whether we acknowledge it or not.

"Monday Thinking"

Bountiful complaints build the week,
Disregarding, the unforeseen opportunity,
That God has stored up for the meek,
And the sinner to surrender unto purity.

Drawing near to daylight like shining rays,
I anticipate radiating, with no negative thinking,
Ablazed inspirational speaking on highways,
I'm ignoring the signs interrupting minutes linking.

Use your Mondays to declare monthly intentions,
Being disciplined, in hopes of a reward to recover,
Let the produce of our fruits plenish all populations,
Reporting the demonstration from a God that hover.

"Bye Past, Hello Future"

Blessed are those whom sins are covered,
The shameful things in which we've suffered.

May we no longer be victims of the past,
When our Lord's provided us freedom at last.

Now is the time to make a favorable decision,
To focus on passions that drive your vision.

Look beyond all the hard moments you face,
And know we all move at a different pace.

Success is not a story told overnight,
If you want it, you must put up a fight.

There is nothing given that's underserved,
But it's up to you to get what's preferred.

"Power of Gifts"

The best is yet to come for those who try...

Never letting excuses overpower their will...

They trust in the Lord, and on him do they rely...

Expecting the best as a part of the deal...

There is greatness in us, no one can deny...

Not limited to music talents, or athletic skill...

But for our separate abilities to rectify...

Our purpose for our nations to heal...

Use your gifts to exemplify how we reunify...

Stop letting deceit be the reasons we kill...

Against all the odds let us stand to defy...

What Satan himself doesn't want love to reveal.

"More Out of Life"

It's a new week full of new opportunities,
Where planning is expressed in creativities,
Just to save up and get out of communities,
That limits your gifts or possibilities.

It's time to use what God has put inside of you,
More than physical attribute displayed by few,
Power and dominion are within us too,
Awaiting the faith to increase in value.

Don't let sports, music, and the love of fame,
Be your focus if you won't change the game,
God has more for you if you call on his name,
Answering prayers, so you're no longer the same.

"Forgiveness is Freedom"

Letting go of the past isn't always simple,
Knowing that your present living is a challenge,
There are memories often hidden within the temple,
Causing unwanted misery that's hard to manage.

Forgiveness comes in due time for healing,
But how can you obtain it if you don't let go,
Like we're entertained by downhearted feelings,
Rather than the process, we take to grow.

I believe everyone travels the road of pain,
Yet we overlook what we inflict on others,
Only if we knew the type of world we could gain,
When were treated equally, as sisters and brothers.

CHAPTER 5

Hope

All hope is not lost...

I chose to give my daughter the middle name "Hope" because that's exactly what she gave me. Wanting something to happen that was truly good, thinking that it would make me happy for a lifetime, the Lord put it inside of me, to birth. We are to cherish a specific desire with anticipation, believing that the Lord will provide. Trusting in the promise of God, that he will give you, the desires of your heart. Delighting in the will of the Father guides us to our aspirations of truth.

Devotions to dreams cause a desire to flame, but God will let you know when you burn and are not consumed. No hope for God will burden you. Light can shine from the inside of you when your desire arises.

All hope is not lost when you believe in the Lord. When you want to give up, God will give you an expectation, for obtainment from the passion in your heart. We are to expect then what we dream with confidence, that the Lord will make it work in our favor, to receive by faith. Any amount of faith is useful when you measure it in God. The Lord will take even a mustard seed, as faith to move mountains. When you put your complete trust in God, he will make all your paths straight, and he will show you the intents of your heart. Only the pure in heart will partake in the promises of God. His children, increasing in hope, to inherit the kingdom of Heaven, on earth.

"Time for Change"

If God's people that are called by his name,
Will humble themselves to pray and seek,
Imagine all the things we could proclaim,
As people reach their predestined peak.

It's time to turn from our wicked ways,
Wanting nothing more than to see His face,
Then will heaven hear us, all of our days,
Forgiving our sins to mend the land we pace.

God's patience exercising our salvation,
Proceeds the moment every child is to repent,
Like the word in action, we will live revelation,
Or later find out why the Bible was sent.

"Smile Through Trials"

There should always be a reason to smile...
Although situations can bring us down...
Thankfully greater is coming after while...

So, keep your head up without a frown.

Every person in their life will face a trial...
And moments when there is no one around…
But you can call on Jesus with nothing to dial...

By praising him with a heart filled sound.

Having faith in Christ isn't everyone's style…
Nevertheless, it is in him that we all abound...
Not only for the believer but also the gentile...

Who was once lost, and with God were found.

"Seeking Godly Truth"

I believe we are reaching a place in time...
Where people are seeking the truth daily...
Stuck in this world trying to make a dime...
And the peace we genuinely want comes vaguely.
I wish I could take back the hurt of the church...
To give people knowledge of their crime...
How the lies put many in a desperate search...
Yet God still has a plan even in this rhyme.

Notwithstanding the word of God travels in the flesh...
Carrying His love so that everyone may see him...
Allow the teachings of Christ to be our refresh...
Using hope as an anchor to counter outer whim.

"Hope in Dreams"

I thought I lost hope in my dreams…
The inward secrets that I vowed to my soul were
the deepest part of me worth seeking…
I'm glad I never let hope escape the gates of my dreams to
grant someone my promise from on high, I deserve the
happiness of bliss, from my youth I had missed…
Tragic tales we all can tell, of the changes that left
us thoughtless, to the wonderment of the future we
once saw arising through years of trouble…
Its a struggle to hold on to visions that don't resemble
the present, hesitant to accept that greatness takes time
to climb the heights of unmovable mountains…
This journey travel through more than valleys when the
sky's the limit, don't plummet your confidence; it's our
mission to fulfill what we see to profit humanity.

"All Things Possible"

We all have had some good days, as well as bad,
There are times you won't rejoice because you're sad.

When situations get rough, it's for you to stay glad,
Thanking the lord daily and making the devil mad.

Success is no senseless road when you want the best,
There will be nights you cry and gain no rest.

Many moments your faith will be put to the test,
And only the durable press on to finish the quest.

With God in your life anything you ask he's able,
Despite how it looks he can prove the imaginable.

If you believe in yourself, you become unstoppable,
Conquering goals the world said was impossible.

"Seeking God Daily"

There is no weapon that won't form against us,

Whether natural or spiritual they come in cycles,

And we can catch satanic plans if we stay in focus,

As discernment guides us directly to our miracles.

God's voice is heard more than we preach daily,

Awaiting to see what his people are praying,

Maybe today seeking him will be the main priority,

To understand His word and what he's saying

Will there be a difference in God's children?

We are to live in conviction to fulfill his vision,

Stop doubting the ability of your most profound passion,

With God, before you, there's no better decision.

"Hopeful Insight"

Hope is more than a four letter word...

It builds a belief that brings about unseen things...

Yielding destiny...

You are too close to quit...

Faltered focusing on the fears of fantasies...

Now believing in what hope has already created...

Meditating day and night for the pleasantries...

From above to make everything right...

Thank God, He has given us an insight...

On how to overcome this fight…

We might fall, slip, stumble, or trip…

Never will doubts for dreams abide...

Faith is far greater than all my mistakes…

I now claim it as fate...it is just the path...

I had to take to make it to where God called...

Me to be for the altering of history...

"Doubting Faith"

I have had my share of days filled with glee,
And I had my smiles taken away by calamity.

But through it, all God has been my resting place,
Gracing me daily for His glory to showcase.

I know what it means to praise Him, all the time...
Whether I'm crying, or trying to do good...
Worship solidified, He is God forever in his prime...
Protecting me from evil, my Robin Hood...

I will lift up His name in any form of trouble,
His power foretold causes my faith to double.

Out of my spirit, I surrendered the doubted seed,
To embrace in Christ what I earnestly need.

"Poetry's My Gift"

If given a chance to go far with my poetry, I would widely spread my love for all humanity...

Inspiring souls to take control of the choices they make, to fulfill their mission on earth, every time we wake...

Maybe I could help build God's army, causing Satan to fear the power I realize lives inside me...

To those who can't see beyond the physical, I can teach to exercise self-control, by targeting the mental...

Surely all who read my thoughts weekly can understand I'm not just religious but deeply rooted within my spiritual...

I just remain true to myself by using faith as my daily inspiration, to be the love someone believes they can receive...

The luxuries of learning have become my lifestyle, and giving to others in prose has become worthwhile...

My gift of poetry I will never return when I can help free people from the pain that burns...

Knowing my gift is exceptional, I vowed to God to never hide what he made of me, by sharing and...

Uplifting love regularly.

"Pain"

If I could take every memory of pain away, I would start with the abandonment of fathers, and oblivious mothers, who can't see past their own feelings, to raise a child. Maybe this would be the start, to restore all the broken hearts, that roam streets but repeat the same cycle and trends preceded before them.

Perhaps I could ask God, to transfer pain to the same person that betrayed your trust and allow them to see how loyalty and honesty are a must.

Or I could get rid of the sin that's known to us as lust, and hope that molesting, perverted hands could never have the chance to rape again. I can't lie I hate this world and all the evil that dwells in the lives of those, who try to survive in a twisted society, who wants minorities to die desperately.

... that's just the way it is.

At what point do we form a unity of one mind, and see how we are one kind of race, declaring that we are human.

...parts of me could care less for change.

Yet it wouldn't be faith if we didn't hope for the impossible.

Therefore put it in the hands of the invisible, and believe with no wavering, He is capable to heal.

Increase your faith...

Increase your faith by taking a chance that something good will happen, from believing in God. Someone may be able to provide you with the help you seek now, but Jehovah is ready to help us for the rest of our lives. We lose hope in man daily, but our faith in God will never fail us. The Lord requires our faith to see his power manifested in the earth. We are spirits made in his image to do great work in the world, and when we believe on the son Jesus, we are made wise with the truth. Our hope in God is for our ultimate benefit. Placing our faith in the Holy Spirit guarantees us victory over every negative force in the universe. The power of God will protect you, and preserve you until the day of Christ return.

Do not allow the evils of this world to convince you that there is no God. The Lord is alive and well. Taking notice of all creation from his throne in heaven. There is no amount of science to explain all the existence of the universe, and yet more people rely on theories than the truths of the spirit. Talk to God for yourself, and see to it that he will welcome his presence to you. The Father wants to show his love to all that search after him. When the Lord is your deepest desire, you will never turn away from his hand. There is no greater love, than that of the Father, our Ruler, and King. Increase your hope in the Lord, and see to it that you will never hunger, nor thirst again. Jehovah is the highest fulfillment there is to know. Period.

"God's Planned Victory"

Eyes have not seen...
Ears have not heard...
Nor has it entered into the hearts of man
All that God has previously planned...

His love of grand magnitudes connected every attribute,
Latitude to the ocean floors...
For the rich to give religiously...
The poor to live prodigiously...
Casting away tortuous conditions,
To grant an eternity of admission in heavenly apparition...

"Beginning of Change"

New depths have come across…
No loss have I found in letting go of pain…
Or fear in keeping pride…
I'm now sane to the change that must…
Take place for the hurt to be erased…

Chased even…
Left bleeding…
Exceeding its timing…

Unwilling, I've left blind my heart to the views of lost paths…
The aftermath was not worth my better half in Christ…

Now love awaits, the fate of my deepest desires in your hands to hold, faith.
Let the new beginning of rarity, lead to never forsaken prosperity, hope.

Above all odds is God's favor…
Improving the wealth of fervor…
To live inherently blessed forever…

"Power of Choice"

The power of choice has always existed...
Like burning desires it acquires interest...
Overtime with no option of expiring...

Yes, my dreams go higher than the expenses...
Of freedom in its maturity for equality...
Life isn't make believe for me....
Choice taught me how to rejoice...
During a storm...
No matter how torn...
I will forever adorn...
The Father, Spirit, and son Jesus...

Through Him, I'm what I needed to become...
Through Him that loves me, I've already won...

No matter the choices made we have the...
Opportunity to take another turn...
And choose well from what we learn...
Being lead by truth to marry peace...

"To the Brokenhearted"

Loss can feel like a neglected road...
Unfairly acceptable in plain sight.

I've heard your sorrow numerously told...
As you fought back the tears with all your might.

Memories of laughter left to be consoled...
Shedding thoughts of who's wrong or right.

I pray for the brokenhearted carrying any load...
There's no way to express the pain at night.

May your healing be in God's hand to mold...
That he would grant you peace in the day of light.

Double for your trouble...

There is double for your trouble when you believe in God. Through trusting in his holy word, we are made known to his promises. The Lord is faithful and just to do as he promised, if he spoke it, it should come to pass. God is not a man, that he would lie. Everything that we lose we gain in double. For the suffering of our hearts, he rewards us with more than enough to maintain. Walking with his children every day we are reminded of his goodness, how his mercy is everlasting, and how his truths endure from generation to generation. The trials that we face in this present times are not comparable, to what is waiting on the other end of our belief in God's power to provide.

As you know, what goes around, comes back around. When the Lord shows up in your situation, the grace of God is coming with him. His grace is sufficient, and the kindness that he has for his creation is steady, that he feels our hurt. Our hope in God is the key to success, portals of majesty behind each door we see. For his glory, we are to receive his blessings. He delights in those who persist after his heart. A real parent indeed unwilling to hold back the riches of his royalty, to unbothering behavior. He is not selfish with what he has hidden in destiny. Try him, to know him for the redeemer he is. Building your hope to experience double, for the troubles of your past. Ask the Lord what you need, and increase your faith to acknowledge the miracle take place.

"Reminded of Hope"

God, I've fallen many times before, I laid in low places that held the weight of darkness, I couldn't see myself lifting.

Yet and still you listened to cries, thinking I had no replies, as answers surrounded me in the form of forgiveness and compassion.

God, I can only imagine your gift of peace… The perfect balance of strength and patience…

I gave up on waiting, to rush into preparations of sin, I could never battle and win alone, I thought I was gone.

Undeserving to return unto your particular place of grace, you showed me, love, with reasons to praise.

I'm sorry I fled from your call…

Scared I'd continually fall, I felt too small to travel the distance of truth you set before me, paving my own way, no wonder I strayed.

In my sinking, you reminded me of hope… Nope. To the words of the enemy.

No longer are you, leading me towards the insanity that paralyzed the faith in me. I'm sorry for doubting…

Shouting in a dance of triumph I'll laugh through the wars to come… because like my spirit spoke to me…

I've already won.

"A Better Way"

Happiness is like a mystical myth...
When disappointments are a roadblock pith.

The power of our faith replaces intersections...
Encouraging us to select new directions.

...For a better way.

CHAPTER 6

Peace

Perfect Peace...

You can breathe easy when you know that God's got it all in control. No matter what the concern is, or what the circumstance may be, the Lord knows the end before the beginning, which we win. There is no loss in God, everything that no longer serves a purpose to your life will always be removed. The mission of Christ is a journey of divine revelation, and when the truth is made clear, we rejoice in the works of the Lord.

Granting us the peace we can rest in the arms of God, knowing our best is flowing directly from the Father.

He wants to give us a feeling of perfect harmony, with our minds stayed on him. Overwhelming gladness of his wonders surfacing. A state in which there is no war or fighting, just the time spent in agreement with the Holy Spirit. Use the harmony of a personal relationship with Jesus, to bring you into the calmness of tranquility, to quiet your spirit. Becoming free from disturbance, wrapped in the security of a holy presence, you can shed your emotions binding your soul. Freedom from oppressive thoughts, and disquieting voices. Choose to form a pact with the Lord, and be transformed obsolete.

"Blessed Not Stressed"

Not every day will be full of gladness,
So, we count our blessings,
Choosing to focus less on our sadness,
So, we prevent life stressing.

Ability to fulfill your dreams lie inside,
When patience becomes your virtue,
Preparing steps that strengthen new strides,
When your future is in clear view.

Don't be deceived by setbacks or failures,
You can still accomplish your inner desires,
Regardless of those barriers and accusers,
You have peace knowing what victory requires.

"Peace in His Presence"

Let this day be full of prolonged peace,
May every door needed become open,
And whatever is wrong God, please release,
Notably, the things left unspoken.
Let His love follow you everywhere you go,
Helping you fill the voids and places broken,
May the blood cover you from head to toe,
Giving life to the things that have yet woken.
Let everything cease, that brings you stress,
To welcome God in and feel his presence,
Know that he has chosen you to bless,
Praise him now, and await his essence.

"No Worry, No Stress"

Why is it hard for us to live blessed...
Ignoring the good, to be stressed...
God told us not to worry about a thing...
Because all that we need, He will bring...
His promises to us are yes and amen...
When delighted in, commandments of ten...
There are times in which you will sin...
But He won't ever leave, not now or then...
Stop allowing Satan the power of our mind...
Call on Jesus, and forget the past behind...
Your life has better days ahead than this...
If you give it all up, for His heavenly bliss...

"Psyche of Positivity"

What if I told you life isn't as bad as we say...
That we have the choice to enjoy our day.

Using the power of the psyche for positivity...
To control the atmosphere from negativity.

Why do people enjoy moments complaining...
More than time spent working, while gaining.

Life was not designed to be miserable...
But, to show you a place far more desirable.

Maybe a hunger for the unknown is the purpose...
To camouflage the fear of being nervous.

Enlightened you can't explain the supernatural...
Until you've been tested to prove it factual.

Cast your cares on the Lord...

Cast your cares on the Lord because he cares for you. There is no greater love than that of the Father for his children. The Lord is our peace and our comfort in every situation of life. No loss of material value can be paralleled to the price paid on Calvary when Jesus died for our sins. Matters of this world will come to distract us from the journey we face. In the time of raging storms, we ought to give it over to the Holy Spirit. Lifting our hands up high in surrendering unto the Lord, we let go of our weights, for the blessing of the saints.

Never hold on to what God wants to tear away. We only hurt ourselves in the process. Everything the Lord wants to give us is to prosper us for the future. In our future, there is life more abundantly, where you can bear fruit in each season. Destiny is limitless when God is the author of your fate. There is no hatred in the Lord, except for evil, and if you are a new creature in Jesus, you are saved from the wrath of God. He wants us all protected from his fire, but we learn to turn our lives over to him when we go through a crisis.

Most loss cause frustration to the mind that generally puts people in depression. When depression sets in, you are now forced to trust on your own will, or you can accept God's will. There is no condemnation in Christ Jesus, and he is ready to lift our heavy burdens if we let him take the lead. This is the perfect time to put God first in your life. And when you lose sight of your direction in this world, he will be the answer to all your problems. Resulting in the perfect peace, amongst the roaring thunders of calamity. Ask God for help, he is waiting.

"Life Is But A Dream"

I guess you can say I believe in fairytales,
The mystical and magical atmospheres,
That creates what I speak, and poof it appears.

I imagine myself as a princess,
On my journey of decorous for Queen status,
Trapped in towers of mental oppression,
Forced into sleep with no prosperous vision.
Tricked for my gifts, in return of silence,
But, blessed with a Godfather and King,
Who saves me from everything.

Why won't people comprehend the yearnings,
We can have are not make believe,
That by the Holy Spirit we do receive.

He Promised to show his mercy and grace.
When your heart is His residing space.
The Lord is willing to replace the emptiness,
Let my life be a witness,
He has more than enough care to share.
If you will open your mind to trust in the,
Possibilities of a love that will always be there.

"Joy Over Pain"

I believe in the joy and peace of others around me,
We all deserve to rejoice in the moments of resting.
Why mourn for the death of an unfulfilled journey,
No matter what we're suffering or internal wrestling.

If we took the time to examine the lives we live,
Many could understand how pain helped them gain.
And the power accumulated to forgive,
Is the freedom existing when we strain through the pain.

Thank the Father above for free will each day,
As you choose this road to steady and display.
Let him know all of the things undesired to stay,
Then pray the joy to come won't be taken away.

"God of Compassion"

I serve a God full of mercy and compassion,
When I fall short of his glory, my sins He forgive.
Allowing me to make mistakes and learn correction,
His death and rising, for me to live cohesive.

Perhaps it's the God in me that seeks his peace,
And why I use poetry, to freely express empathy.
Hoping it will help a troubled heart or mind increase,
To be more like Christ, in showing others sympathy.

We as people have an opportunity to form a unity,
Yet we lose sight of the real problems unchanged.
Overlooking what causes the inward deformity,
It becomes easy to see why many are estranged.

"Oh Peace"

Oh peace, where are you?
The soul yet trying to rest, as our free will is,
Always put to the test...
Despite tiresome efforts, we continue to press
Forward settling for less, by giving into stress.

My goal is to live blessed!

Oh peace, what are you?
To most, you are tranquillity, in the midst of a,
Mental typhoon...
To others, you are a treaty, in the heat of battle
Zones consumed, of doom.

My goal is for your rescue soon!

Oh, peace, who are you?
I know you as the risen savior, who came to set,
The captives free...
The Trinity made in one, (Father, Spirit, and son)
Who won the victory, over the enemy.

My goal is to be with you for an eternity!

"Let God Take Control"

There's nothing that seems to bring me peace...

Like starting over...

To know that I have a chance to advance in a new...

Direction of a far greater plan...

Even when I comprehend little, my faith says...

I win from the beginning...

Hopefully, it will allow me to see the blessing in the...

Face of temporary misery...

Unfortunately, everything isn't easy to maintain...

And with patience, there's much to obtain....

So I'll try harder not to complain when I endure...

Strain while stretching towards my goal...

I now realize the grand prize in letting God...

Take control...

With Him, I'm never alone...

The captain on my team, I can never go wrong...

As long as He is first...

Lord complete what you started in me…

So that I, May be used for your glory...

"Trust in the Lord"

Trust in the Lord with all thine heart every day,
Submit to Him your feelings whenever you pray.
As God imparts counsel for right directions to go,
Even when He requires of things, you just say no.

It's unacceptable to settle for the role of the victim,
When you can be the victor living with freedom.
How many chances must we be given to change,
Before we witness the blessings put in our range.

The Lord is near to calm the tears of our fears,
He's awaiting our quietness, that we can hear.
It is the heart in us all that He always notice,
God grants peace when you're used for his service.

PART IV

Loneliness

Why does loneliness come?

Loneliness comes to remind us that we need people. Everything about human life is related to connections and communication, which are reciprocated infinitely. Without other people, it is impossible to expand the plans of God. As children of the Lord, we are to unify with one another, not only to give him praise and reverence but also to help.

The Father uses every one of us to speak his words, to show his love, to share his blessings, and to bring peace. It is our duty to our brothers and sisters in Christ, to do the will of the Lord. People do not become famous by themselves. Countless people choose to elevate the gifts of man, yet when the Lord exalts you, it is to make his name high in the earth, not your own.

Loneliness is a deceit of the enemy. You may feel as if you are alone, but I assure you that you are not, alone. God is omnipresent and always in your presence. The Lord is still near, no matter where you are. Trust and believe that he knows everything about you, and all that concerns your heart. God is able and just to do as he said, never doubt that he will show up for you. During seasons of loneliness, you are to reflect on the plans for your life. Sometimes we underestimate the time that the Lord allows us to build.

Alone time is necessary to grow. You need to hear the word of God at all times. There will be times that the Lord will step in, and he will help you gather your thoughts, you get to rest, and you find peace. Don't forsake his kindness for misery.

"Positive Karma"

I've heard beauty, is only skin deep...

The best of you is on the inside...

Uniquely assorted, it's of excellent keep...

Revealing why some are never satisfied...

Let's spread love to those, we do not know...

We all have something, we're going through...

If we treated people better, we all would grow...

Whether a few words or a smile, it's up to you...

Do not let this weekend, without one change...

Every day there's a chance that we can improve...

How we talk and act towards others, let's rearrange...

To accept higher in exchange, for what God remove...

CHAPTER 7

Love

God is...

God is love.

"Love of Unity"

Where two or three choose to gather...
God is in the midst…

Declaring together, more is accomplished.

Unity is an unspoken answered truth...
Yet we sabotage our need…

For without love, how can we be freed?

See people as the helpmates they are...
Connecting your purpose …

For us all, to live more capacious.

"Spread Christ Love"

If we showered strangers with kindness,
And the broken-hearted with less apathy,
We could see beyond our own blindness,
One day onward to developing telepathy.

We all go through struggles that need care,
Yet we look past the troubles of others,
When moments we want someone to be there,
To show us love like fathers and mothers.

So many demand high measures of respect,
Failing to realize how they affect everyone,
Life will always produce a different aspect,
Therefore value experiences with no shun.

"Real Love"

Love is a word that is hard to find...
Watered down to be based on how you feel,
Neglecting the truth we've turned blind...
Desperately hunting to witness what is real...
Love is patient, long-suffering, and kind...
It does not envy, boast, or stand proud...
Keeping no record of wrong in mind...
Reflecting in action or words are spoken aloud...
Love is what Jesus Christ's death defined...
Demonstrating compassion for God's creation...
That we could be what He designed initially...
Embracing one another across every nation...

"Jesus is Love"

If I told you love was a metaphor,
Would you understand what for?
Not a hug, or kiss, nor sex, or word,
But, the promise no man truly deserved.

Love was altered through sinful eyes,
Suspecting what others know to be real.
His existence rewritten, portrayed by lies,
Yet for us, we still seek for Christ to heal.

Jesus is love there's no meaning without him,
The reason slaves were carried on in hymns.
Our patterns of life made clear beyond belief,
God's son was the perfect piece for our relief.

Love conquers all...

We all should know the feeling of robust and constant affection for a person. The attraction you have felt for a person romantically. Tenderness uncommon, you're overwhelmed by its ability to control you, to do good. I know love, and I know it truly.

My life is full of love. Love from my family. Love from my friends. Most importantly, the love of my Father in Heaven. The Lord loves me, and he loves you, too. The God of all creation does not hold back his love for us. Covering the multitude of sins, he sent his son to the cross to die. The love of a Father, sacrificing an innocent lamb for the rest of the world, for an everlasting paradise. Amazing! There is no greater love.

Love conquers all evil. Love is the mastering of hate. When you love like God, you can love people past there hurt, and your own. You force out the memories of the past and trade them for the faith in a better future. Do not keep allowing Satan the power over you, through your door to the past. In this journey, you will walk alone, and you will have people alongside, of you all the way, but you can not enter Heaven by two. In this world, we answer to the Lord for ourselves. We can hope for the best in all of humanity, but only a few will change their ways to make the world a better place, through the power of the Holy Spirit. In doing so, we will see the wonder-working power of a true and living God. Through the spirit, we are not consumed by the darkness of this world, because we know that we hold the light. Love drives away all negativity, challenging the enemy to prove our victory.

Love is warm, an assuring empathy, to sympathize with who I

am, respectfully. To tell me, I'm due to your affection for endearment. Knowing a beloved person, the object of attachment can show the same devotion, or admiration makes love easy. An unselfish loyalty and benevolent yearning to fulfill the concerns of another is good loving. The same fatherly care from God for all humankind. We should be able to show it in our brotherly adorations, daily amongst nations. Personifying the God in our hearts, we can help the poor, heal the sick, care for the fatherless, and the widows. Treat others, the way you desire to be treated. It's only fair. Love always comes back full circle, waiting to be accepted by a made up mind to hold on tight. There is no loneliness in love. Love conquers all.

"Trust Worthy Christ"

Trust in the Lord till the fire, of your core, emerge,
Setting the ablaze of praise, to an uprising surge.

Christ you are grand in your significance, oh Holy one!
Who gave himself, to free us from what we'd done.

My Father is a healer and the author of time,
Nothing is inconceivable, He exists in his prime.

Our three in one that Satan simulates in six,
My God, My God, your name, we cannot nix.

Whenever we fall, your solutions solve them,
Jesus, you are the answer to everyone's problem.

"Cleansing Water"

God loves us beyond our daily faults…

Through repentance and patience, He saves.

Examining the heart to bring sin to a halt...

He delivered us to be, the water we crave.

Oh, taste and see that the Lord is good...

The well that never runs dry. He is a billow.

A refuge in distress where danger stood…

Jesus is my secret path, in winch He I follow.

Let this same love of Christ be also in you…

Worshipping the Lord in spirit and in truth.

As strangers approach to let them see it too…

Leading them to a God, that is full of sooth.

"Love One Another"

Love one another as you, desire to be in theory...

Be not like Cain, whose anger was untamed,
That he could kill, His little brother unashamed.

Why must we continue to relive past history?

Today we witness the same hatred and evil,
That keeps minorities, from entirely living civil.

We were commanded to love with Christ in us...

Was enslaving each other, first not enough,
To show black on black crime leads to cuffs.

Let us not love by words, but actions as a plus...

Obeying God until, everyone's last breath,
Dissemination as our obligation, unto death.

It's give, and take...

In love, there will always be give, and take. There is no way around not sharing when it comes to love. Whether it be your time, eye contact, or simple words, you must give and receive. Letting your heart be open to the vulnerabilities that come with heartache, that drew you into loneliness. Love makes it possible to believe in the power of healing. Love erases the sting of the past, with memories of a greater affection.

We are all deserving of love in any form that it shall come. In trusting the Lord, you follow the path of his words, to find what is for you, permanently. Know that in love, loneliness will only make room when something is lacking. Our needs can not be met by just one person. That is why we answer to God. The family will disappoint you, friends will let you down, but God will send the right strangers in your life to assist you when you need it the most.

God is not limited to resources, and he has every vessel on earth he needs, to be used by his will to see about you. Help is available with faith, no matter what you are up against. The Lord delights in the heart of a cheerful giver. There is nothing that he will not do for the likes of you. Giving is a real sign that God is working. Love is always seen in action, delivering to the masses what is most desired. Just like love, to know the matters of the heart.

Connecting with God to renew the right mind, that the soul would flourish in any time of sadness, or loneliness that arises. God is full of surprises, witnessing every thought you think, he is in sync with all of you. As you grow in faith, the signs of his love will manifest all around you. Trading spaces with your hurt, to accurately convert your spirit, forever.

"Transparent Beauty"

Why do people feed into the pressures of being jealous?
Removing the lens off of self, many instead emulate.
Blinding themselves from the reasons to be zealous,
Their image is made skewed, manifesting in self-hate.

There is nothing wrong with appreciating your beauty,
When God chose for us to be, who we are physically.

Keep in mind things you do to defile the body,
For we were bought, with a price to live spiritually.

Let features of the natural be made invisible,
That the love of God will reveal what is internal,
Transparency we will see in all the makings of a miracle,
In which looks can't compare, define, or mislabel.

"Better Half of Love"

I forever sit and dwell on the memories of a family...
And friendships that will never end.
I don't think many people understand the power...
Of a spiritual and mental bond, that seems only to be,
Expressed outside of a romantic connection.
I love how my passion for love travels beyond the...
Question of shared blood,
I know there's more to it.
Diversity travels through the veins of the letters...
That form the one word that has more,
Explanations than an addition equation.
Still, we can't seem to solve, the problem question...
Determining the difference between them.
Love is more than we make of it,
Yet only a few know, the better half of it.

"Love Truly"

One day people will translate, God is love truly,
Going further than simplistic, teachings of affection.
Let it be of truth in its entirety, to bring clarity,
To restore souls of passion, with no condemnation.
I wish more people would forgive and teach another,
So that hurt from the past, could no longer last.

Enabling the heart freedom, to find another lover...
But many don't heal, they just move on too fast.
When we have a foundation, of Christ, we know...
That His road to Calvary was the ultimate victory.
Our love is everything positive, in life we can show...
Ending the opportunity of negativity to overtake unity.

"Nothing Without God"

Where would we be without the creation of God?
What would we see if it were not for His imagination?
Nothing.
Who can birth His own life, and take it in
Death as a full demonstration, of love to the nations?
The same God from generation to generation.

Why do many live in fear, but yet refuse to hear
The word pray, when that is the primary way,
We can know what the Lord has to say.
Maybe one day, people will believe.
Faith many had before, was indeed a gift God allowed
Them to receive.
It seems that only some are willing to seek and yet,
It is the meek who will inherit the earth, so yes
Christ is worth the sacrifice of your life in full.

God desires the praises of His children, to bestow
Upon them the wonders of His glory and the
Comfort of His mercy, His grace is sufficient and
His power is proficient, in any circumstance.
With perseverance humble in His presence,
Knowing now, for yourselves the favor
Of His coherence.

"Thirsting for Love"

Love is such an imaginary scene…

Full of grandeur that gathers the means

Providing what we think to be security…

Misleading impurity to shield insecurities

Ultimately surpassing attention, we're thirsting…

Intrusions of cooperation on the heart are a given

When falsehood decisions keep our love driven…

Sipping on the mediocre left dripping for more

Like craving water desperately at the seashore…

We're merely wanting to float with no bitter taste

Bias to a chase, every relationship will be a waste…

"Speaking on Love"

Love.

If I could take the time to rewind, pause, and fast forward...To find and combine all

there is to know about you, maybe...Then I could enjoy you, perhaps I would not ignore

you...But explore you, and adore you as I've often seen others do...

Love.

You don't seem to come in a ribbon tied package, however...I've seen you reused and

cleaned up for the next person...Who didn't think to abuse the trust you kept inside of

you...A different point of view was exposed when the self-control... To wait for you had

no debate...

Love.

Many seek and never discover what there is to know of you...More than money played

hands, and finger pleasured dances...Romance is temporary, but your bond never seems

to leave...Or neglect the space it created in the mind...

Love.

So why do they hate you, recreate you, and isolate you, when...All you tried to do was

bring joy with peace into a place...In need of harmony...

"that's simple to me because they did it to Christ and any who follows thee..."

"Sharing Love"

What is the definition of love?
I'm starting to get the concept that the,
World knows little about it,
When for centuries we have still grown to these,
Make believe stories and fantasies,
Created to depict emotions, with no devotion of,
Checks and balances,
Romance is sweet, but there's more to becoming,
Husband and wife.
Interesting love is expressed, in the same depths,
Regardless of a title, or bloodstream,
Yet we seem, to only acknowledge love in,
Accordance with relationships, and tiptoe pass
The instructions, of Christ.
Love your neighbor, like yourself,
No matter the color, of your sister or brother,
One day fathers and mothers will teach this
Command and undivided we'll stand,
Chasing thousands, to millions of demons,
Let my poems, be more than inspiration, but real
Love demonstrations, reflecting unity from above,
Please finish what He started, by sharing the love,
Or in the end it'll hurt us, that's why forgiveness,
And trust, along with faith, is a must.

"God's Pervasive Love"

It was your pervasive love that kept me
How you knew my every move and thought
That brought me to my knees
Every plea you heard
Every tear you observed
Your grace abounding in truth became
My reward
Lord my God, Jehovah my all
Adoration and reverence, Oh, how I long for
More of your presence
Jonah's rebellion flattering my opinion of
Right and wrong
Disobedience harmonizing depressions song
Until mercifulness came along
To render for my surrender your unfailing
And pervasive love
He loved me...
He loves me…
He love me.

"A Love Letter"

Love letters often come together in a spectacular matter,

When my thoughts have stayed on you.

Not only do I unravel verity,

There is wisdom gained in variety,

Love has no perfected form unless I dress it,

With your essence.

I admire the sight of you,

Spiritually coherent …it's apparent,

I'm one with you.

Forgiveness flowing effortlessly I cry out yes,

To be blessed by your desire for me,

Fluently my tongue utters praises to keep you up,

Raised in my heart. You are the ancient of days,

Numbers have no measure,

To the pleasures of your favor.

You love me so, I pray this love always grow,

I'm yours to hold and never let go,

Walk with me in the secret place,

Excite in my soul intimacy,

Balance the defiance of my alliance with sin,

To meet an experience deep within.

I want to be made whole by you,

Perfected knowing you chasten those who are,

Loved beyond daily faults,

You taught me how to love from the root,

With your pursuit of my life,

You illustrated sacrifice.

Body…mind…and spirit I submit to you,

Not of my own, I commit, all to subdue the flesh,

Rescued from my mess I worship,

In the presence of your grace,

That keeps me in your dwelling place,

I can never find in my visual reality,

Thankfully, I carry the unchanging serenity,

Promised to me that you will never leave me.

"Thoughts of Romance"

Mental stimulation holds for more value…

When pertaining to the likes of me…

Can you articulate your words creatively?

While arousing the spirit inside of me...

Presentations of debonair romance love affairs...

Become a blur when you don't know...

What I prefer...

Assumptions killed the player when he made…

Determinations without learning from mistakes...

How many times must a woman anticipate...

Transparency inwardly...

Life's mind-boggling when you're lacking intimacy...

If real love carries security...

It's still foreign to me...

I just hope when it visits for the last time...

Perchance it will increase the ability of my rhymes…

Cause my heart, and theirs to align…

No shame in lovemaking shall we find...

Power of patience becoming our ally...

No need for lies and alibis...

We'll comply...

To rely...

On love.

"A Vision of Love"

I chose to love you.

To be the one you think of daily...

Yep, the one you call baby.

Maybe it's the respect, shown both in public...

And when we're alone.

I'm mind blown, that I feel you...

Could it be God's pull of what is true?

There are prayers He's answered...

I never spoke aloud...

But, somehow you resemble them in the flesh.

Yes, I believe.

Perhaps now I can apply more faith towards...

Monogamy and one day appreciate a love...

That God brought out of me.

No longer will my dreams be a fantasy...

It will be my turn to receive.

Erases will cross my brain's cell held in captivity...

Of past males that smeared stains over my heart.

There will never be a part of me with availability...

To deliver undying devotion when...

Ours will last an eternity.

That's how my mind speaks, of romance to God...

I know the love I cherish, will one day flourish...

While others try to discourage, what they don't know.

Never will it perish if my creator is the author of fate.

So, don't hate when it comes to fruition...

I'm just writing my vision.

CHAPTER 8

Relationships

Communication is key...

In any relationship, communication is the key to its survival. People all over the world speak a variety of languages, and in every culture, we as humans have evolved through our communication, and still, we struggle to comprehend change. Conversation brings us closer together through reasoning and understanding. I value the power we have to speak our thoughts to others, but I must admit the frustrations I have when I cannot get along with some of the personalities of this world. People are not the same, and we do not think alike. That alone makes it challenging to build relationships, but with patience, we find how rewarding it can be, talking to others.

Communication is how you strengthen any relationship. Opening up your mouth to tell your story, not only teaches someone else about you, but you learn more, of who you are. Clarity is prosperous when more people take the time to focus on someone else, just as much as they do themselves. Assuming that we are all made equal, it is a true expression of poor communication. Many dreams are waiting to soar, but many will never be accomplished because of oppression, and a lack of initiation. Intentions speak for themselves, and proper communication ensures truth.

"Resilience While Lonely"

I often pray for those who perceive they're alone,
To help them see, we are not on our own.
One reason God created woman from man's bone,
And later sent Jesus down from his throne.

Don't get caught up in people who leave,
Realize there is nothing left to retrieve.
For benignity in portions, you have to grieve,
Accepting the truth no longer to be naïve.

Not all relationships will work the same,
Some teach us what's inside we need to tame.
Others may result in guilt, blame, and shame,
But God's love for you aims to remain.

"Call to Order"

I've been requested to write many poems in difficult times...
However, little may come, to make my fingertips run to the tip of
my pencil, that can truly get people to change...
When anger has a deranged frame of mind that needs to unwind,
for me to penetrate the core all the more.

Silence has not killed us all, but with violence, we fall…
We should have evolved from jealous retaliation, all the while we're
producing generations and nations of hate…
Many can't relate, to the downside of history when you cover your
eyes, to hide the mystery of manipulative genocide, revealed from
racial pride.

Prayer is all I know, as many of our ancestors did for them to pull
through...
However, the skin is not a curse nor my reasons in life to fear what
shall appear in the future….
People are created to fight for what's right or equal, let's just learn
from the original, to produce a better sequel.

"Accepted Differences"

Social media has become a feeding frenzy for knowledge,

Lies hidden in the comments of replies...

Who can understand what's real, when it's disguised so well?

Yet we try to tell, everyone how they should live...

And then pretend that it brings rationality,

To the problems we face.

But race is the primary debate of every,

Underlined message we repost the most...

What can you do when people dislike themselves?

And allow it to transcend on to others...

With boldness behind keyboards, and phone screens,

Hatreds have been seen from the earliest procreation...

And this country struggles with implications,

To advance a population that can accept differences of appearances...

Past disillusions that dark is evil and bright are right.

Let no peace, be a statement of helplessness,

However, the way to reciprocate the love for...

Hate and allow oppression its place behind,

Rapes, beatings, and killings that try to break...

The barriers of serenity.

Many will never stop to even hear me...

I'll keep praying rapidly that eventually...

We will advance from this spiral of iniquity.

"Ostensible Freedom"

I hope one day people will comprehend forgiveness,
And not take it for what the world calls weakness.

That we will be able to admit what's reprehensible,
Allowing ourselves true freedom that's ostensible.

"More out of Love"

Many look forward to one day finding love,
Feelings from someone their thinking of,
That particular person that values what you do,
The kind of bond shared between just two.

Are there people today who still want more?
More than a temporary pleasure to explore,
But one-day marriage, and possibly a family,
While others rather be players living in solitary.

Relationships have lost their identity today,
Causing more pain, and children are to pay,
Hopeful we as people learn from the past,
Or keep accepting things that'll never last...

Power of unity...

The power of agreement is strong enough to break curses in any realm of life. The agreement is the very essence of God. Being unified as three in one, Father, Holy Spirit, and Jesus, we can possess the earth from evil, by spreading the love of good.

Building relationships, we stop the attack of loneliness in its tracks. Let us bond together in love, to seek the will of the Father, that we may know life more abundantly. Through unity, we will live blessed and victoriously. Being in full agreement with the Lord, combining to be apart of his glory, and mighty works.

One in Christ Jesus...

There is a condition of harmony when you are on one accord with the Lord. Having continuity of blessings with no deviation, or change from your purpose. God delights in the unification of Christ in our situations. In the time of loneliness never neglect to call on God. Looking below from the Heavens, he is ready to turn our frowns upside down, into a smile, full of his splendor and care. He is always there, we just have to believe. Receive in your heart that Christ Jesus is Lord. The same man who walked this journey of life, battling sin, to deliver us all. As God the Father was with Christ, the son, he is with us, speaking his word into our minds, to be seen with our very eyes.

One with Christ, is the best price for a life of prosperity, with no sorrow. He holds the answer to every tomorrow and will anoint you never to borrow, knowing he is the supplier. Jesus is the way to take us higher. Trust in his plans, that he has everything in his hands. All relationships come in its proper time, do not rush Gods timing on love.

When Jesus has your heart, no one can break it. Just be patient. God is moving on your behalf.

"Need of Equality"

We are living in a troubled hour of lies,
That fuel desperation and destruction,
Where good and evil are the battles we face,
But have yet to find healing to replace the hurt,
Filling the space in the hearts of man…

Can we look past the sins of men to see,
There're not many things that separate us,
Other than our trust in the Lord.
We need to use the Word of God to relieve,
Not to break down the spirits of individuals,
To prevail over the shallow thoughts of race,
And take the time to discover,
The purpose that exists on the inside…

Pride will be the killer if we don't humble,
Ourselves to the facts we don't know everything,
Let those wise with knowledge be who rise to,
Stop the violence so we can teach and preach,
God's eternal inheritance.

"Fight for Generational Change"

When hatred prevails over acceptance,
Jealousy and imitation are a new alliance.
And right has become the outsider,
As bad does well to deceive the best for less.
Why are we killing each other right in the streets?
We fail to remember these are the residences,
Which those are supposed to sleep,
Yet they wait for death, to rest in peace.
This is not acceptable. Not in the least.
Still, plenty continue to teach children,
How to pick up a gun for fun,
Ignoring he has free will to kill,
Whatever makes his immature emotions set flame.
This is not a game! We can not keep giving way to,
Murder as though it's something you will easily let go.
What if it was you!
Your family! Your friends! Will it ever end!
Why fight against one another when God's command,
Was to love our sisters and brothers as ourselves.
We cannot continue the suppression of speech,
If voices are what impacts us to be reached by each.
Holy spirit arrests every hand, I command that they,
Surrender unto you, whatever you want them to do
In Jesus name, Satan, this world is about to change.

"God for Yourself"

There are so many that refuse to believe,
In a living God full of everything to retrieve.
Adopting us from the hands of our enemy,
In order for us to live a life full of prosperity.

Don't let his love be limited to holidays,
When you need him to make all your ways.
With darkness surrounding he covers you,
Forgiving every sin when you ask him to.

Value the spirituality, not the religions,
That is now manipulated today by demons.
God is more than a one-day morning show,
But without a relationship, you'll never know.

"Important Bonds"

There are many moments to enjoy in life,
Most are filled with family or a friend,
That causes us to avoid the enemy's strife,
For Heaven to be rewarded. Transcend.

Never neglect the power of bonds made,
The same people who came to your aide,
And spoke your name whenever they prayed,
The relationships you wouldn't want to, trade.

Don't ever give up on the ones you love,
Because we all are prone to make mistakes,
Especially when its push comes to shove,
But God uses it for the glory of his, namesakes.

"Child Development"

A parent plays a crucial role in a child's survival,
Whether you acknowledge it or not.
No kid chose to endure this world of a bitter rival,
But you're responsible for what is taught.
Openly mother and Father will have to be audible,
Seeking the Lord high above the heavens.
Developing your rule book of what is behavioral,
By illustrating his love for us as heathens.
Don't let pride be the reasons you're not accountable,
Children are affected by decisions.
Focus on their primary needs to instill their cerebral,
Prepping their way to provisions.
With greater expectations, of God's working miracles.

PART V

Forgiveness

Why do I need to forgive...

The lack of forgiveness is a symptom of brokenness, manifested overtime with no successful closure, to heal. Forgiveness is necessary for our personal growth, ceasing to feel any resentment, we choose to remove the anger, towards another. In hopes to maintain peace in our hearts, it is our responsibility to make our situations known to God. Consciously cautioning our hearts, we are to surround ourselves with those who have our best interest in mind. It is hard to forgive, but we learn the lessons of heartache, to protect us from the mistakes of our past. When we forgive others, it heals us from the inside. To make room for God to turn the circumstances around, for the benefit of his favor.

It takes time...

It takes time to develop a sincere heart to forgive. Not all hurt causes the same damage, and not all wombs travel as deep. Inevitable pain requires a longer time to heal, and in that process, it is crucial to reach out to those who hurt you. In other cases, it's best to delete some people with no warning or hesitation. Investing the efforts in yourself to mend your broken pieces, will open the window of opportunity for God to do the rest. Rejoice in advance for the rebirth of your peace, accepting the scars that you take each day, as reminders to turn another way. No pain you experience will be wasted when you use your patience, to graduate towards better decision making. When you know better, you do better.

CHAPTER 9

Prayer

Ask, and you shall receive...

A conversation with God is all we need to make our path straight. Through prayer, we can ask the Lord whatever we desire to know. During prayer, we commit our will to the Father, to be conformed into his likeness. During the tough times of life, we rely on the voice of the Lord to lead us in the way, we are to go. Prayer is our source of communication with God, which ensures us of our purpose, in each day.

When we pray, we ought to ask the Lord for his forgiveness. He is full of love and will not hold your past sins against you. Forgiveness of man in our hearts, brings forgiveness for our souls, in the sight of the Father. Jehovah is just, and he will not forgive you of your faults if you do not forgive others. His love for all humanity is distributed equally, whoever he blesses, he also forgives, and when we repent with our whole heart, there is no condemnation left to feel.

With a mind to forgive, like God, we eliminate the presence of bitterness, that produces hatred. The upright in heart shall inherit the kingdom of God, sealing their name in the book of life. Denying the urges of this world, all negativity will bow, as you resist its energy to sin. Then you focus on the positivity in your life, so prayer will align things, for the good of your faith.

"Need of Prayer"

There are so many things wrong in society,
That it is hard for people to find what's true.

Government, churches, and schools failing,
So now what do we as believers try to pursue?

Racism rising and bodies falling to brutality,
Dividing the nation and destroying family,
As prisons make minorities the majority,
And no one seems to believe in Christianity.

Our world is struggling to find peace today,
Wandering in darkness without a clue.

What more must come to cause us to pray,
Before we turn to God to fix the issue.

"Prayer of Peace"

There are things in life that will affect us,

We don't always know why, or how it happen,

But it's vital that we don't lose focus,

As God uses trials, for our faith to sharpen.

I pray the Holy Spirit of peace to transcend,

Removing every doubt and worrying nerve,

Lord hear the cries of the hearts to mend,

As forgiveness substitutes what we deserve.

Lord give us your heart to love just like you,

With the strength to make it no matter what,

But above all help bring understanding too,

Knowing it is you, and not a feeling in our gut.

- Amen

"Prayer for the World"

Our Father residing in the heavens let your will be
Done above and below
Let your presence be free to reign in every
Domain both big and small
Lord let your love shower leaving no more room
For dry places
Fill our temples with joy where there are empty
Spaces, and help us fight off evil when we become
Impatient

Jesus this world needs your help today, so I will
Look to you with great faith every time I pray to
Heal the sick and broken
Father restore anything taken and bless the hearts
Who hurt from words unspoken
You are more than able to turn us away from sin
Giving us a sensation in you
Lord do what you must to gain the unbelievers' trust
So that we will provide you with praise for the rest of our days

Amen

"Prayer of Justice"

Father, I come to you humbly, as I can seeking your
Presence in a dying world...
Asking you to protect and provide for your,
Children in a society that refuses to hide its,
Hatred and animosity...
Lord, you said you would be our refuge in the,
Time of trouble, but the deaths we see continue
To double...
My Lord, my Lord you said, you would never,
Forsake us but God, we have yet to receive,
Any justice...
Lord, I cry out for every broken soul that can't,
Control the tears they cry,
Holy Spirit we need you, to move in the midst of the,
People to fix what we try, to do on our own...
Lord, we know you can do no wrong, yet many have,
Given up on your power, before your final hour,
So Jesus let your will be done, today on earth,
As it is in Heaven...
Release blessings, and miracles for the people who,
Need it most...
From coast to coast, let praises rise into the sky as smiles,
Cover our faces removing every frown, the devil uses to,
Keep us down in Jesus name I pray...
- Amen.

"Prayer Filled Praise"

Father God, I thank you for being the awesome
And powerful being you are
The Heavens and Earth reverence you whether
Near or far because of your mercy
Your compassion is limitless despite the sin we
Profess and display everyday

No one can take your name from our lips when
Worship erupts from within
You are a dear friend to the end, and there is no
One above or below in which you withhold love
Lord don't let our faith in you return unto us void
But make it be deployed for your glory

Jesus, there's no one greater, and I pray that you
Speak to us sooner than later
Comfort us in our darkest hours sending rain
Showers in the form of blessings
We need you to right every wrong and eliminate
Whatever Satan tries to prolong

Let your will be done, as thy kingdom come
Amen

"A Call to God"

Each night before I sleep, I stare out of my window...
At the stars hidden behind the placement of shallow,
Trees and make pleas beyond the charcoal sky,
Awaiting your reply...
I know our eyes have, had many evenings of...
Poker face dealt hands, and I spoke much life,
Demands yet you called my bluff, every time a,
Tear ran down my cheek...
God, I can't lie to you when everything right never,
Dwells in darkness, and I can't help but wonder...
Where is your light when I'm in trouble,
Can I only be dreaming...
Maybe I fell asleep, during another prayer,
Before you could speak,
I no longer want to reap what I've sown if,
Depression is my comfort zone.
Or is this how Job felt when he was living right...
And yet in your delight, you mentioned my name,
To prove to Satan through pain,
I would remain the same...
I thought living for you would help me,
It seems to hurt me at times, even more than the world,
In my weakness, you are made strong,
So God, why are you taking so long...
I'm desperately holding out from doubt,

Because I know my heavenly Father,

I can't live without...

God as your faithful servant I need you,

To please come see about me!

"Prayer for the Fallen"

All of me?
I don't understand...
How do I give it to you?
When my attempts have failed before your,
Eyes repeatedly...
Secretly desiring my wants, with the likes of you,
I admit it's hard to love as true...
All, not some. Not, a little. Not, a bit.
Somehow that doesn't always sit well when I,
Rather dwell on the pleasures of temptation,
That divides my heart from yours.
It doesn't sound fair-spoken aloud, but how can
I lie to an all-knowing God when you created,
My simplest entities...
An unforgettable sacrifice that gave all of you,
In place of me.
Sorry is never enough when you asked for,
Mine in return...
My wrongs covered with blood, how can I not,
Love such a God...
My will is never as strong to prolong,
The fight of evil, so I know I need you...
I just pray today, not to fall.
However if I do,
Lord knows that for you, I'd try again...

Forever gathering my all, I'll call to you for assistance,

To stay in your presence...

And I say be praised, all my days.

Amen.

God hears us...

God hears us all whenever we seek him in prayer. Everything on this journey of life, is for an expected end, with Christ Jesus. Through a personal relationship with Jehovah, our prayer time will increase into new dimensions of revelation. Seeking the Lord with no doubt, but with fear and reverence, we excel. It is for us to prevail.

Expanding in wealth, and the riches of his name, we have hopes going forward.

Each trial we tread upon has its own individuality, to be made known in the earth. Let the power of forgiveness for both yourself and others set you free. There is much more in life to expect, that is full of goodness, so make a choice to surrender to God. Pray that those who hurt you will become more like Christ. The same creator that made all of the world made all of humanity, and it is our job to pray for their change.

Prayer has the full capacity to deliver the saints and the sinners when we lift them up in God. Never have to worry, our faith is resting in the will of the Father. Give your all completely to the Lord when you pray. Believing that the outcome of your hopes will manifest in this present world. Igniting your passions for more, pray until you hear from the king. He will be ready to tell you everything you need for an incredible destiny.

EPILOGUE

In closing...

God is real, and he desires for us to know him. I have learned to love because of my Father's teachings and his compassion for me. Through a relationship with Christ, I have obtained the wisdom, I need to travel this journey of the divine. Putting my trust in the Spirit, I'm walking by faith, and not by sight. Take value in the present, repenting for the past sins of your life, and accepting the plan of God. In the Lord, we are free to live with no worries or insecurities, the world may press. Though trials, and tribulations of all sorts, may approach, be steadfast in the will of the Lord, working through you. Be patient to endure any pain. For we are built to conquer in this world. It's for you to discover what has been hidden within the journey ahead. Being spiritually fed, may you find everything in your heart spoken, and unsaid. Be Blessed.

Discussion Questions

11. Do you have a favorite poem? If so, Why?

12. Who is someone that inspires you throughout life?

13. Does reading the poetry inspire you?

14. Has your life journey been what you expected?

15. What are the chapters of your life triumphs and struggles?

16. Which chapter could you relate to the most?

17. Did you disagree with anything? Explain.

18. Was there a change in your thinking after reading this book?

19. Would you consider reading a poem every day for inspiration?

20. When you read the poetry, how does it make you feel?

21. Where do you believe your journey is leading you?

22. Why is inspiration important?

www.ingramcontent.com/pod-product-compliance
Lightning Source LLC
Chambersburg PA
CBHW021634120626
46545CB00002B/539